If I Were an Animal

IF I WERE
AN ANIMAL

Compiled and Illustrated by
Fleur Cowles

With a Foreword by
H.R.H. Prince Philip

William Morrow and Company, Inc. | *New York*

Library of Congress Cataloging-in-Publication Data

If I were an animal.

1. Celebrities—Psychology. 2. Animals—Miscellanea.
3. Fantasy. I. Cowles, Fleur.
CT105.I3   1987   920'.02   86-18035
ISBN 0-688-06150-8

Printed in the United States of America

First U.S. Edition

1 2 3 4 5 6 7 8 9 10

BOOK DESIGN BY VICTORIA HARTMAN

Foreword

As its name implies, World Wildlife Fund is in the business of raising money for the conservation of nature and to that end Fleur Cowles - a long time and dedicated supporter of the Fund - has offered a proportion of the royalties from the sale of this book to WWF.

It is easy enough to feel an affinity to a particular species of animal, but I just wonder what it would be like to be reincarnated in an animal whose species had been so reduced in numbers that it was in danger of extinction. What would be its feelings towards the human species whose population explosion had denied it somewhere to exist and by sheer indifference had destroyed any chance of it finding a mate and producing a family? There are not just a few such species, there are a great many and the list is getting longer every day. When I look at the shelf with all the volumes of the Red Data Books listing endangered species I must confess that I am tempted to ask for reincarnation as a particularly deadly virus, but that is perhaps going too far. I would much rather see the human species voluntarily restrict its numbers out of consideration for the rest of the living world with which it still has a chance of sharing this planet.

H.R.H. The Duke of Edinburgh, K.G., K.T.

Contents

If I Were an Animal

Introduction

I have always been besotted with animals, and so has most of mankind since time began, even when man and animals were natural enemies. Our affections and imagery are overrun by them—in art, literature, politics, and commerce. Animals have been sculpted, written about, portrayed on canvas (something I do in my own paintings), caged in zoos, petted in homes, eaten for sustenance and chased on land, sea and air for game.

Animals adorned pottery. They were effigies in gold, brass and clay in the Third World, were dreamlike images of the Far East, the allegorized part of the fable-maker's and story-teller's bag of tricks. They haunt man's dreams.

Thus, it is neither surprising nor eccentric of me to ask over one hundred world-famous personalities to imagine changing places with one in their "next lives." "If you could be reincarnated as an animal, what would it have to be, and why?" I asked. Quite a few answers were written in verse, all mirthful. Others expounded in prose. Among them you meet some extraordinary surprises!

Animals became important in the Golden Age of the Garden of Eden. Man, even before recorded history, worshiped them, eventually, as gods. I wonder what the earliest man (who painted such magnificent beasts on his cave walls) would have wanted to be (if his mind could even have grasped the idea of an afterlife)—the deer he hunted for food?

A quarter of a million years later, would the effete moguls also have chosen the same deer to immortalize the grace and beauty they so admired? Would Romans have chosen the lion? The Egyptians a cat (or other animal god, perhaps the scarab, which has survived as a national symbol)? Would Cleopatra have liked to come back to haunt her enemies as an asp? Would Benjamin Franklin return as the rattlesnake he actually preferred to the eagle as a national emblem?

In royal and other portraiture, animals were an essential ingredient. Kings, queens, and princes (especially children) were never painted without their pets (Velázquez comes to mind). The early American primitive painters of children went from family to family with nearly finished paintings to which they added head, face—and always a pet (birds and dogs were the favorites). Nineteenth- and twentieth-century adult portraits include birds, cats, monkeys, deer, peacocks, cavalry horses, and cheetahs—often the props of folkloric and anecdotal canvases. Mice, butterflies, hummingbirds, insects, even snakes, invaded the flower masterpieces of Dutch painters. John Ruskin, referring to Edwin Landseer, said he endowed his painted animals with human characteristics, that his dogs were cynical, coy, and comical or noble.

The pioneers who settled the Americas braved such things as huge bison with humped backs and hair like a lion's, killer bears, deadly snakes, and even alligators to the south. But by the mid-nineteenth century, the battle against the wilderness was won; many animals that terrorized colonists assumed more benign characters. Edward Hicks, in his remarkable series of paintings called "The Peaceable Kingdom," symbolized this by assembling an extraordinary bestiary of the wild and tamed living together—as he presumed God expected them to do.

Today, animals are household pets, taken for granted (sometimes to the exclusion of children). They are the signs of the zodiac; they equate goodness (the lamb) with evil (the snake). They are part of our vernacular. Bulls and bears have moved to Wall Street to define market conditions. England's Lloyd's Bank identifies itself by a black horse, Exxon the tiger, Leyland Motors the jaguar. There is the Greyhound bus, Hong Kong's Tiger Palm, Elsie the Cow, and bulldog paper clips. Pubs and inns use animal signs (often horses and swans) to lure patrons. Athletic teams like to be known as the Lions. Animals are also partnered to politics: we have the British lion, the American eagle, the Iranian lion (brandishing a prophetic sword); the American Democrats use the donkey as a symbol, the Republicans an elephant. Hawks versus doves tells us about man's attitude to war.

We are described as eager beavers, buck- or rabbit-toothed, henpecked, loan sharks. We are badgered, birdbrained, dogged, dog-tired, dog-eared, worm-eaten, catlike, catty, cool cats, catburglars, kittenish, slothful, fish- or hawk-eyed, little lambs, pigeon-toed, culture vultures.

We give bear hugs, weep crocodile tears, take catnaps, travel at a snail's pace, make beelines, have snake hips and ponytails. We are as quiet as a mouse, crazy as a loon, bald as a coot, busy as a bee, happy as a lark—and proud as a peacock. A "pig" is used sneeringly for "the Law"; militant women use it for men in general!

The fact that birds top the list of choices by my contributors brings to mind a little-told tale about Benjamin Franklin, who fought a losing battle to use the rattlesnake (instead of the eagle) as the symbol of the new America: He insisted that it—and not the eagle—should go on the flag of the emerging Republic, to shout "Don't Tread on Me" in defiance of British colonial policies. Franklin, it is said, even suggested sending a shipload of rattlesnakes to England's St. James's Park, Spring Garden, and other places of pleasure (particularly noblemen's gardens). Such thoughts fled from his head when he later came to live in London and grew to love his British friends. Today, the eagle is still minted on American coins and adorns official buildings (the largest must be on the American Embassy façade in London).

Sir Yehudi Menuhin (who practically lives in the air)

probably synthesizes the many reasons for longing to fly like a bird: As an eagle, he could view the glorious panorama he loves to see below him from an airplane—without running the gauntlet of ticket-counter queues, crowds, questioning, cross purposes, and the general mayhem common to all airports. No hijacking either, I add.

The choices are great, varying from a seagull by a duke who always nourished the dream that he is a human glider to a house martin, about which Lord Carrington has written a poem. José Mayorga was torn between the two and chose a tiger instead of a bird.

Dog-lovers (I am one) will be glad to see that they are second to birds in popularity—and for endlessly amusing reasons. Jilly Cooper, who identifies herself as a mongrel, wants to be one; Mary Quant, who sees the world through the fringe of her own hair, obviously chose to be a sheepdog!

It's not surprising that dogs turned out to be second to birds as choices, since it is said by many that the best thing about man *is* his dog. One wit once remarked that the only reason a dog has so many friends is that it wags its tail instead of its tongue. They are often man's only companion; they also guide the blind, go hunting, keep guard, and in one of the coldest great houses of Ireland they sleep on the feet of guests to keep them warm.

Most reasons given for wanting to be a dog (and, yes, a cat too) are in order to live the same cosseted life as their own pets. Nancy Holmes identifies her Jack Russell terrier as a very-small-and-built-for-action package of black spots on white. America's chief of protocol wants to be as full of love as huskies are and her husband wrote a poem to agree with her. Karl Lagerfeld, who dresses the world's most luxurious women, dreams of being a dachshund, but it must have humor.

The cat brings flashes of museum collections to my mind,

especially the Egyptian rooms at the British Museum, where, to me, the most handsome goddess of all is a cat. Poems, including T. S. Eliot's, have been written about them (his eventually became the musical *Cats*). And not so long ago, Mark Twain wrote that if one could be crossed with man, man would be improved, but the cat contaminated. Their independence and cruel selectivity to human companions suggests that they have read his remarks! They grant favors only when it suits them. They are beautiful to look at, but evasive about returning your affection. Your glances can be ignored. They fall asleep instantly, outraging many of us who cannot! They live in beautiful surroundings, but pretend they are in the jungle and treat your home as their own private territory. Beware the cat if you are a new dog!

I must be wrong. The Brazilian ambassador to the Court of St. James's wants to be a home cat. Elizabeth Emanuel (of the husband-and-wife team that designed Princess Diana's wedding dress) says CATS have the most PURRfect lifestyle, can go out of doors if CLAWStrophobic indoors, and for a little sport, CATch birds and then PAWS to get their breath back. She has written a whole CATalog of other magical reasons.

The cat has prehensile claws, can jump nine times its own height, can see in the dark, is completely self-reliant. Fans of the cat suggest God made this animal last.

It's delightful that six others prefer to be a dolphin/porpoise —from a news-magazine bureau chief to a Broadway producer, a *Vogue* editor, an ex-USA ambassador, to TV explorer-documentation Julian Pettifer who says that if he were one, he'd be able to explore the earth under his own powers "looking up at human creatures in their tin cans." Anyone at sea, whether in a dinghy, yacht, or ocean steamer, who has been followed by smiling, frolicking dolphins (which Bonnie Angelo describes as "the mammal/fish at the crossroads of sea and air, of man and beast") must love them. Logbooks record that they guide ships through unsafe waters.

The ape is something else again, inspiring humor as well as admiration. Lord Dudley's poem ends with: "So thanks to Fleur, when next you see one in the zoo, it may be me." Two beautiful women want to be gorillas: Twiggy, that tall slim bundle of energy and many talents in the theater, hopes to be a massive hairy primate with sad eyes. Clare Francis, who sailed the world alone, sees the gorilla as a human baby needing protection. Their potential ugliness as gorillas cannot worry these two; they will certainly be the most beautiful primates in the world.

The bull comes off next-best to an unlikely pair—appealing to the female head of the world's most successful model agency, to a social commentator, and to my husband, who looks his own new bull in the eye with a feeling of mutual respect. Only two wanted (and not too enthusiastically) to be horses (perhaps the biggest shock in a book with so many British contributors).

Ned Sherrin, who claims he has beautiful legs, would like to multiply his assets—as a centipede! Two wish to be fleas! One, a film critic and author, ought to want to become one to revenge the makers of any awful films he has had to review—though this was *not* his reason. The other, one of the world's most famous action painters, Georges Mathieu, simply has to be read to be believed! But one must remember that Beethoven wrote a song about the flea he adored, dressed up, decorated—and made prime minister of the government—all to the consternation of his own wife!

If you could come back as a bacterium, you'd be able to start a new and better world, says Monaco's consul general. There are even (and I shudder) a little brown snake and a boa constrictor (to make Raquel Welch an endangered species); and a sable, the pterodactyl, mute swan, salamander (if you're lazy by conviction), an aardvark (to be first in the animal telephone directory!), anteater, crab, and pigeon are among other personal dreams.

There are, too, a panda, a unicorn, the old gray donkey of *Winnie the Pooh* (with its noble, melancholy dignity), and a giraffe who'd give a golden-voiced opera singer much more room for her voice to expand. Two butterfly ladies wanted to be real butterflies, another a cricket. Marc Bohan, fashionable Paris couturier (Christian Dior), sees himself as a fox. Another ambassador will become a sable to enhance beautiful women (at the price of being skinned!), another, a furry little coati, like those found roaming the Amazon, with their mischievous curious ways. But no one chose to become an ordinary fish. What a pity! A fish could go home and lie about the size of the man he got away from! No one wanted to be a bear, on whom our greatest passion as tiny children was showered. I hoped someone would want to be a warthog—to me a really ugly animal who doesn't know it, and struts and behaves like a movie star. Good nature (a lovable one) must come high on the list of respect for inherited characteristics—so many wanted to have one.

Author James A. Michener not only would like to be an armadillo (which he finds "an adorable creature") but he fully expects to be one shortly after his death. Two others join the armor-plated brigade, as tortoises: Douglas Fairbanks, Jr., and BBC's David Dimbleby. An ermine, bejeweled, regal, and snow-white, is the Victoria and Albert Museum director's choice. The Loch Ness Monster strongly appeals to the great dancer Wayne Sleep of the Royal Ballet and Theatre—because, although always televised and filmed, the monster has never had to perform or appear!

Prince Sadruddin Aga Khan wants to be that custodian of the Antarctic, the emperor penguin, for many erudite reasons (but also because it is always impeccably dressed and never needs to pack a dinner jacket for travel). BBC's Sir Robin Day says that though he's been likened to many animals, he has at least been spared comparison with the orangutan or the skunk.

Who wants to be a rat? I do, says Ian McCallum, director of the American Museum at Bath—"because there is a very good chance they will survive when the human species vanishes."

Editor of the handsome *Connoisseur* magazine, Thomas Hoving, contends that "no creature but the otter packs so much beauty, strength, grace, cunningness, speed, agility, intelligence, and familial concern into such a small gorgeous frame." Naturalist Dr. David Bellamy loves the sea otter for its splendidly idyllic life he describes so well.

The magnificent greater kudu of Nigeria appeals to Chief Edu, admitting that some of its characteristics may unwittingly bear similarities to his own. Landseer's magestic lions on Trafalgar Square, with their protection to nobility, appeal to Viscount MacMillan.

My own choice wasn't difficult after I got one dream out of the way. If, like the others, I had a free choice (which I haven't because my conservation-oriented conscience would interfere) I'd long to be a beautiful butterfly (hopefully, a fragile specimen) darting about in the short, precious life allowed me—between the flowers in my own garden which I love so much. Flying wouldn't be difficult. As a girl, I often felt I was as able to fly as any bird or butterfly—just by flapping my own arms (a temptation I squashed by the greatest self-discipline).

But no. Having done my share of swooping about in little and very large real planes, including the Concorde, today I console myself by leaving the business of flying to these machines. Being by nature and activity a conservationist, I had to choose an endangered animal. If this be my fate, let it be the elegant, handsomely dressed cheetah—from one of my own paintings. As the fastest animal on earth, I could fly over the ground at sixty miles an hour, dedicated to outwit the poacher intent on turning my spectacular fur into a coat for some thoughtless, uncaring lady.

I must end with Victor Hugo's words from *Les Miserables*: "Animals are nothing but the forms of our virtues and vices, wandering before our eyes, the visible phantoms of our souls." If this be so, what have we in innocence revealed?

Fleur Cowles, 1985

Brian Aherne

Actor, and wife, Eleanor

I hope I shall never return to life as an animal! Some are useful to mankind and some nice to look at, but they are all devoid of our possible advantages: history, art, music, powers of invention, dreams of the future or knowledge of the past. We can come to love some of them—puppies or kittens—but I still wouldn't want to be one.

My wife, Eleanor, on the other hand, wants to be a giraffe—I rather think this is because she thinks I resemble one, towering over those around me.

Bonnie Angelo

Bureau chief,
Time magazine, London

ᗆ

A difficult decision, this. First I thought I'd like to be a butterfly, wings drenched with color beyond any palette, sampling the choicest blossoms, hang-gliding in the summer breeze. Or maybe a rhinoceros, hulking head lowered, horn menacing. *Then* there'd be no more jostling by photographers armed with camera gear obliterating the clear view I've staked out for covering, in my role as a fly on the wall of history, events featuring president/prime minister/ queen/*et al.*

But no. When all is considered, I must be a porpoise.

From the time I first met one of these sleek creatures face to face, I on the dry side of the Marineland tank, he flashing a watery smile from the other, I was lost, bewitched by these rollicking, frolicking mammal/fish that live at the crossroads of air and sea, of man and beast. I grew even fonder of them on an Atlantic crossing when a veritable porpoise navy escorted our ship through days of unrelieved fog, like reassuring swimming coaches encouraging us through a dismal, unwinnable race. It was a reminder of all those tales—some maybe even true—of porpoises as gentle guardians helping the lesser species, *homo sapiens* when he is in trouble in hostile seas. (On second thoughts the ship was jammed with students, stacked in layers in every nook and cranny; the porpoises might have thought, less altruistically, that they were on the trail of the world's biggest sardine tin.)

There's so much that gives porpoises a special place in the

animal kingdom: their lively conversations with each other (who know what stories they tell?), their dazzling talents as performers (they clearly relish the crowd's applause as much as their fish rewards), and through it all their unfailing good humor. Playful, helpful, brainy, beguiling—who could ask to be more the next time around? No offense, butterflies and rhinos, but you'll have to wait.

R. W. Apple, Jr.

Bureau chief,
The New York Times, London

⚬⚬⚬

Not a lion—I haven't the dignity for that. Not a leopard—I lack the grace. And certainly not an eagle—I have already seen plenty of human folly without the benefit of a bird's-eye view.

No, I think I should come back to earth as a Jack Russell terrier. It would please me to be a mongrel, and the Kennel Club thinks so little of the Jack's antecedents that it refuses to recognize the breed. Alertness and tenacity in full measure, qualities I think I have on my better days; loyalty, a quality I admire over most; and a never-failing sense of humor. A good loud bark, always so handy.

Maybe I could go into the circus—lots of Jacks do—and that has always seemed a good line to me, as much fun as journalism; and they teach you useful things, like how to jump through hoops. Maybe I could even learn to put one ear up and one ear down, the way a Jack I used to know could; he was called Frederico Barbarossa, and he took his name seriously. I think I would probably call myself Charlemagne.

Stanley Arnold

Author, financial counselor

The operative word, as Rudyard Kipling himself might have put it, is "if." *If* there is another life after this one, and *if* in another life I could return to this earth, and *if* I could return only as an animal, then what animal would I wish to be?

An anteater? I could make a fortune renting out my services at picnics. With the world as it is, the best way really to return would be as an *ostrich* with a long neck and a lot of sand. A *crab?* Instead of fingers I'd have claws. How handy that would be for getting out of a crowded bus. A wealthy widow's *cat?* When she died she might leave all her money to me, and then I could be rich and purr at the same time. An *aardvark?* Certainly I would have a preferred listing in the phone book. An *octopus?* It would mean the achievement of a lifelong ambition—to be able to scrub my back in the shower and not miss any spots. An *alligator?* I'm afraid that's not my bag. A *boa constrictor?* I could wrap myself around anybody I wanted. That would make Raquel Welch an endangered species.

All of these lives would be interesting, but I guess I would just rather be a *parrot*. I could save a lot of lives that way. You've heard of coal miners using canaries to warn them of danger. Well, a canary can only warn you to get out. A parrot can tell you which way to go! Being a parrot, nobody would eat me for dinner. Nobody would take me for a walk. I wouldn't have to forage for my food and I would live such a long life that there would be ample time to figure out what I would like to be in the next life.

H.E. Mario Gibson Barboza

Brazilian ambassador to the Court of St. James's

⌇

I can think of no animal rather than the one I already am that I would choose to be in a new life. Certainly not a *man*, of that I am sure. Man is, by far, the meanest of all animals, besides being so irreparably ugly. It suffices for us to note that man has no tail. Now, I ask you how can *any* decent animal go around without a tail; how can it properly express a feeling or a sentiment without wagging its tail?

A dog? Never! How could I ever wish to be an animal so undignified as a dog? Let me just remind you that a dog is known to be man's best friend! Now, let me ask you: How can you trust an animal known to be man's best friend? I'll say no more.

A horse? An elephant? A donkey? No, please, I cannot have any respect for animals that let themselves be just used by man.

As to birds, butterflies, and the like I must grant you that some of them can be quite graceful, even beautiful. But, dearest Fleur, such fragile, inconsequent, irresponsible creatures they are. No, really, they don't count much.

To sum it up: Let me come back, in a new life, exactly what I am now: a home cat. Mind you, not a jungle cat, not even a street cat, but a plain, true, honest *house cat*.

I know no nobler animal. We house cats know our business; we know what we want; we know how to keep our dignity, self-respect, and freedom. No inconsequent, unnecessary running around like a stupid dog. No! We move only when it is absolutely necessary, and then with poise, elegance, balance, with our tails up in the air. No barking for us, no, madam, we known *when* and *how* to use our voices. Above all, no licking man's hand; we know better than that.

For pride, beauty, intelligence, grace, wisdom, character I know no other animal like a cat, a *house cat*. That's why, in answer to your query, I repeat: Let me come back, in a new life, exactly what I am now.

Marius, the Cat

P.S. Of course that is not my real name, for a cat will never tell his true name, "his ineffable effable effanineffable deep and inscrutable singular Name" (see *Old Possum's Book of Practical Cats*).

Betty Beale

Syndicated columnist

My first thought was—why not a racehorse? I have spent my life racing from one event to another, prancing up double staircases of embassies with mane flying and nostrils quivering to sniff out a story. As I like class—and not just a touch of it either—I naturally opted to be a thoroughbred racehorse. But as I pondered the pleasurable pastime of nosing out competitors at the finish line it suddenly occurred to me that I would be indubitably whipped by man in the process, and eventually, perhaps, end up on his dinner plate. Having survived life with neither such experience so far, I scotched the idea.

Next, I decided it might be divine to be a tropical bird—a lovely thing which soars in beauty from its cliffside nests in idyllic, sunswept places like the Virgin Islands. Free as the air and not preyed upon by anything, it trails its long train of white feathers like some undulating veil of chiffon—a vision of effortless grace such as I have loved to imagine myself portraying while dancing hundreds, if not thousands, of miles in Washington ballrooms.

But is there laughter in the life of a bird? Can it chuckle, at least inwardly, over the funny things performed by its feathered friends or comical, paradoxical mankind? And a life without laughter is unthinkable. Besides, I have never been able to handle a train with aplomb, and although I have laid many an egg without meaning to, I am not sure I'd want to do it on purpose.

So, after considerable cogitation I believe—and only believe because how can one be sure in changing the very element in which one lives—that I would like to be a dolphin. I flipped the first time I saw Flipper on television. The joyous expression it bore at all times, its free and graceful cavorting in its liquid playground, charmed me beyond measure. Also, I came finger to skin with a pet one in the Florida Keys when I met Betty Brothers, author of the children's book *Ra-oo and the Porpoise.* Her porpoise—which was really a bottle-nosed dolphin—swam in a big tidal pool walled off from the ocean. Holding on to its fin, Betty dived and leaped and frolicked with it, getting it to roll over and "stand" at her command. It cooperated with relish, tearing off independently when it so desired. It was lovable, responsive, friendly, and levitated with a grace Baryshnikov would envy.

Oppian, the ancient Greek historian, wrote that to kill a dolphin was second only to murdering a human being and anyone doing so, as well as everyone under the same roof, would be unclean and unable to worship the gods. New Zealander Frank Robson, one of the world's experts on dolphins and whales and the author of *Strandings,* which tells

how to help the beached ones get back into the sea, has such an affinity for dolphins he can communicate with them through mental telepathy.

Dolphins are playful and remarkably creative in their play. In at least one dolphinarium they have been trained to think up a new game every day. Having attended during the past forty years an inestimable number of receptions bearing singular resemblance to each other, I am speechless with admiration for such originality.

And, lastly, these enchanting mammals are the kindest, most thoughtful, most altruistic finned things in the world. Traveling as they do in schools (or a pack of relatives, maybe?) they cheerfully help each other with their newborn and against a deadly enemy. They also come to the rescue of humans floundering helplessly in the briny deep, holding them up so they can breathe air and protecting them from killers of the sea.

Doesn't such a highly intelligent, well-meaning, kindly, gregarious animal sound just right for a reincarnated me?

Dr. David J. Bellamy

Conservationist, TV
and radio personality, author

꩜

A sea otter, please.

Why? Because they live in the cold clear waters of the Aleutian Islands, in among giant seaweed. They sleep on their backs in the water with their arms folded across their chests and anchored to a piece of seaweed. They eat shellfish, including the succulent abalone, which they obtain from the bottom complete with a stone to break the shell. I would like to be a female sea otter. They come on to land only to have their babies and then return to the sea, teaching them to swim and fend for themselves. They anchor their babies to a piece of seaweed. What an idyllic life—if only we would leave them alone.

Sir Isaiah Berlin

Author

When asked what animal I'd like to become I could only think of a penguin, but I cannot say why—except that I feel very much like one.

I like the way they move (very slowly). They paddle. They are timid.

I feel the deepest sympathy toward them and their way of life.

Bernhard

Prince of the Netherlands

⤳

I am not yet certain whether I would like to be an elephant or a horse!

I do love both (and then of course I also love dogs), but the first two have preference.

The elephant, like the horse, is a very intelligent animal; both, with few exceptions, have a very good character and are gentle creatures. I feel an affinity with both and I know that both animals seem to recognize me after we have "met."

I have had many experiences to prove it. Once, when I was filming an elephant, it half-charged and suddenly stopped when I talked to it. The next day—and for the remainder of my days in the Selous Reserve—it came to visit my tent every morning. Each time I talked to it. The same thing happened with yet another elephant—years later, in a park in Botswana (one that at first upset the other tourists in the camp).

As for *horses*: I once bought a show jumper from the Japanese. When I gave it some sugar, it turned its head and tried to bite my hand. (Had the Japanese been somewhat cruel?) Soon after, it began to take sugar from my mouth! Later, I sold it to a Canadian and I saw it again in New York when I went to see some stables. The horse recognized me at once and took the sugar from my mouth. Several years later, in Chile, the same thing happened again!

As an *elephant* I cannot decide whether I should be an Indian or an African one. To live in the wild or to serve human beings? And as a *horse,* I know I'd like to jump or race.

As you can see, it is a difficult choice!

Molly Bishop

Portrait painter

⁊✕

Zeus took the form of a swan in order to ravish Leda—not an easy feat, one might think, considering the striking differences in their anatomy. Certainly an excited swan displaying is a magnificent sight—Leda could not have failed to be impressed. Perhaps, as Jupiter is in my birth sign, the wild swan—that creature of fairy myth and Olympian legend—would be an appropriate choice!

Furthermore, swans live in Arcadian landscapes on lovely stretches of water. If bored with the scene, they can fly wheresoever they please—enjoying the way the music engendered by the wind filters through their pinion feathers—a sound like ghostly organ chords, if you have ever heard it.

They mate for life, produce charming downy offspring, and give endless pleasure by their beauty and grace, their noble and dignified mien adding luster to the appearance of many a stately home as well as humbler but no less enchanting ponds and rivers.

Provided one could avoid the unwelcome attentions of predators in the nesting season, and the fiendish, mindless, incomprehensible cruelty of vandals, plus the poisonous lead weights of anglers, a wild swan should achieve a tranquil, enjoyable existence—a reincarnation almost attractive enough to lure one away from the Elysian Fields, should one have been admitted to those celestial regions!

Earl Blackwell

New York social commentator

I was born under the sign of Taurus, so I have always associated myself with the bull. When I set my mind to a goal nothing will interfere until it has been accomplished. Since I am mild-mannered and easygoing I suppose I would like to come back as Ferdinand the bull.

Bill Blass

Fashion designer

Since most animals (except dogs) are endangered, I would love to live again, dangerously, and be a snow leopard.

The beauty and mystery of this animal (and its rarity) would be a rewarding return (even if I did end up on someone's back!).

Philip Bobbitt

Professor of law

I have struggled with your question and would have quit answerless but for a sighting the other evening, here in Texas, of a brown eagle. He reminded me precisely what it is I envy in all animals, and how profoundly we are apart from them. It is *perspective*.

Of course this is much emphasized in the case of the eagle whose remote and lofty vantage point we can never share, even when flying an airplane. For we are going somewhere, are concerned about something (the plane itself, perhaps), while the natural scope of the eagle's thoughts is wide, timeless, and sublime. Connection appears for him, between towns and regions, waters and mountains, that thought has separated for us. Mr. Burroughs once wrote of the eagle, "I would be as far removed from the petty cares and turmoils of this noisy and blustering world." And so would I.

Marc Bohan

Designer-director,
Christian Dior, Paris

➳✕

If I come back, which is less than likely (maybe once is enough!), why not as a fox?

He is handsome, wild, proud, clever, but above all, cunning. He fools everyone! This I like.

The fox in the tale does not produce "victims." He ridicules silly creatures! This I also like. He is invisible; he knows how to hide away and just see without being seen! This I like.

He is beautiful, skillful, sharp (never mind if others do not like him)!

A huge wild pack (dogs nearly his brothers but slaves!) will be necessary to pull him down.

And then he finishes quite beautifully: as a divine scarf wrapped upon a beautiful lady's shoulders.

There is only one danger: to fall into a distasteful designer's hands who will dye his fur in red or yellow. It is the only horrible fate that awaits him.

Victor Borge

Musical satirist

Invited to return in a new life as an animal of my choice, I must delay a decision until answers to three questions are available:

1) When? (Not available to return at the present!)
2) Which species will by then be extinct? (In this life I am often referred to as "one of a kind." In the animal world I may find that distinction less enjoyable.)
3) What fur, skin, hide, scales, and/or feathers will then be fashionable?

However, I do hope for the fair opportunity to postpone my reappearance until brutal scientific and medical experimentation on living creatures has been relegated to the past.

In any case, should the requested information be available, my choice would be an animal of the mammal species. Because, as much as I adore fish, fowl, and others that propagate by laying eggs, having on occasion laid a few myself, I should prefer not to make that a habit.

Helen Gurley Brown

Editor, *Cosmopolitan* magazine

I would choose to be a cat—preferably a Siamese cat. This seems like such a banal and clichéd choice—I wish I could prefer to be the herbivorous orangutan or possibly a frisky sea otter, but it seems to me *nobody* leads the sybaritic life of a beloved kittycat. That would be part of the deal . . . not to be an alleycat or some pitiable creature in a city pound but probably a *Park Avenue* cat who is adored, cosseted, catered to, and utterly spoiled.

Liz Carpenter

Women's-rights campaigner, former White House press officer

I want to come back as a lovable female. I don't want to come back as *any* animal—except a female person who can be a great president of the U.S. and a great lover all at the same time. I hope that qualifies as a mammal creature.

The Rt. Hon.
Lord Carrington,
K.C.M.G., M.C.

Secretary general, NATO

The problem you pose is a difficult one,
needing thought, application and care—
how to retain all the friendship and fun
who to choose from the "Animal Fair."

I think on the whole a *housemartin's* best—
a gregarious and amiable bird,
decently housed and soberly dressed
an admirable chap—in a word.

He travels abroad in the dark winter days
but in summer and spring he won't roam.
I think I would like his style and his ways
and I'd nest in the eaves of my home.

Barbara Cartland
Author

If, in my next reincarnation I become an animal, it will mean I behaved very peculiarly in this life. However, I like Pekingeses because they are so individual, independent and proud—just like me.

After they were given imperial rank in China, when the concubines produced girl babies, which were put on the roofs to die in the sun, they fed the Pekingeses instead. So Pekingeses have human milk in them; this is why they are so intelligent.

Twi-Twi, my white Pekingese, is the first real dog who has ever appeared in Madame Tussaud's; all the others are made-up fancy dogs. He also has a novel, *The Prince and the Pekingese,* named after him. He, therefore, is entitled, like my heroes—invariably dukes—to be very conscious of his own consequence.

> A dog will come when he's called,
> A cat will walk away.
> But a Pekingese will do what he pleases
> Whatever you may say.

Sir Hugh Casson

Architect, former director
Royal Academy, London

The idea of animal reincarnation is difficult and frankly not very appetizing. Horses, cows, and sheep have to sleep rough in cold fields. Whales get slaughtered. Moles bite the heads off worms. Butterflies live only for a day or so. Admittedly cats manage to make themselves comfortable. Swans stay happily married. Corgies can depend upon regular meals. Everybody is happy to see a ladybird. . . .

But only one non-human, it seems, takes time off for a conscious interest in what things look like—the bower bird—adorning its habitat with carefully chosen and meticulously arranged patterns of colored stones, bright petals, or flashing fragments of tin and glass. Anything that has the leisure to worry about pleasanter things than survival surely must be a happy creature, and to live as a bower bird would be worth a try. At least there would be something to talk about.

Jackie Collins

Author

I believe strongly in reincarnation. And I have no doubt that my return to earth will be as a leopard. I have such a strong feeling about leopards, and my house in California is full of paintings, bronzes, and china ornaments (some of them life-size!) of leopards. Once, a long time ago, someone gave me a leopard coat. Every time I wore it I got the strangest feeling, and found I couldn't wear it comfortably. The thing I love about leopards most is their power, freedom, and style. If I have to go, it's the only way to come back!

Jilly Cooper

Columnist

The only animal I really identify with, and that I think is anything like me, is a dog—probably a rather rotund, jolly, slightly unkempt mongrel that bounces up to people wagging its tail, that barks a lot when its territory is threatened. If I came back as a dog I think I should like to live in our house because all the dogs lie on the sofas, creep into the beds at night, get much more expensive food than the humans, and have a bar of chocolate every day for elevenses and at least two long walks a day and endless cuddles. I think I'd quite enjoy that.

H.E. Sergio Correa Da Costa

Brazilian ambassador
to the United States

My first thought went to the sloth, a tree-dwelling mammal of proverbial sluggishness, not uncommon in tropical America. It is a remote cousin of the armadillo, with a round head, inconspicuous ears, flattened face—in fact everything is inconspicuous about the sloth. It camouflages well among the leaves, and its greatest aspiration is to be left entirely alone and unnoticed, never to be bothered. After my own labor-intensive life, a leisure-intensive incarnation sounded very enticing. No wonder! The sloth in Portuguese is called *preguica,* an equivalent of *lazybones.*

A second thought, however, overcame the first.

I definitely would prefer to be a sable. As you well know, it has a very special destiny—which I should like to share: the enhancement of beautiful women.

When elegant sable fur is wrapped around the shoulders or torso of a woman, she has the feeling of being still more glamorous. Of course, I would first have to be skinned— yes, but for such a good cause . . .

Roald Dahl

Author

I would like to come back as a swallow, swift and graceful, swooping and gliding, with all the sky to fly in and with no enemies in the world. I would spend winters in warm North Africa and summers in Europe, nesting and rearing my family each year in the same cosy place under the eaves of a house or in a barn.

Sir Robin Day

BBC TV presenter of political programs

Have I ever imagined myself as one or other of various animals? The answer is no, but other people frequently have. In the course of my television career, I have been likened to many creatures, including a frog, a mongrel terrier, a fox terrier, a bull terrier, a bull, a grizzly bear, a badger, a gnat, a horsefly, a pig (of the male chauvinist variety), and (by Miss Jean Rook) a rattlesnake. I regret to say that I have never inspired comparison with noble creatures such as the lion and the eagle, but at least I have been spared comparison with the orangutan or the skunk.

Michael Denison, C.B.E.

TV and stage actor

⤳

I would be a dog—provided I could be a labrador, living in the country, the pet of a doting *her* and *him.*

Her main duties would be to provide me with regular meals—*not* tins—appreciate my subtle sense of humor, and give a flattering display of relief when I return, relaxed, filthy, and un-run-over after responding for a mere couple of hours or so to the call of the wild—a basic necessity for a dog like me.

As for *him:* I would expect two good (i.e., exhausting) walks a day, rain or shine—preferably the former, which reminds me of the land of my fathers; though the midday sun with my Englishman provokes no fears for my sanity.

Being put on the lead would be a source of friction, particularly when the moon is full and a fox is barking up in the woods or when I want to see off one of those Tutankhamen jobs with yellow eyes; but occasionally it would be a comfort to be escorted across a busy road, or prevented from joining battle without loss of face.

I would enjoy welcoming their guests with a slobbery cushion or shoe—preferably one of *hers* which fit my mouth a treat—taking cover when the yakety-yak level begins to assault my ultra-sensitive hearing.

My darkest hour would be when *they* fill up those awful suitcases and abandon me. I would be unappeased by the arrangements made for my welfare, or by the maudlin love-in—with extra tummy scratchings—that precedes their departure. On their return I would show them! After a perfunctory tail-wag and the ritual offer of a cushion, I'd go off on a protracted safari myself.

My other principal need would be sleep, best conducted between their feet on a king-sized bed where I'd be tolerated except on special occasions. I would require a daybed in the kitchen too, from which to keep a close watch on the preparation of their food and wine—no nonsense about living rough in a kennel.

I would not be expected to work at anything except at being a dog—a full-time occupation if I am to fulfill my potential. And what a potential! Just consider two of my advantages over the human race—and perhaps especially over the theatrical profession.

My range of facial expressions is far greater than theirs, thanks to independently movable ears—which can be worn one forward and the other laid back. Again, in suitable conditions, I should be aware of the approach of a female at a mile's range. (Alas, poor Casanova and Don Juan!) Of course, after the thrill of the chase across country, she may turn out to be no better than an old bag; but even so, with a courtesy rare among humans, I'd hide my disappointment and frisk around her until she felt like the belle of the ball.

Yes, given the right circumstances, a dog's life could be very agreeable. And, if things didn't work out—well, it wouldn't be for long.

David Dimbleby

BBC TV political commentator, publisher

Are animals anything like we think they are? Imagine choosing to be an elephant and finding that they suffer from amnesia, or a rat, and discovering they are naive. So I have chosen an animal with an obvious advantage: the tortoise. It lives longer than we do. It has a very hard shell into which it can retreat in perfect safety while keeping an eye on the world outside. They say that if it is turned over it cannot get back on its feet again, but I do not know whether this is true. I watched a tortoise this summer climbing a steep bank of rock and sand and it seemed to keep its balance quite well. So I shall be a tortoise, though I would like to check on its mating habits before making a final decision.

Kirk Douglas

Actor

If I come back in a new life as an animal—let it be a dog's life. To me friendship is one of the most precious elements in life. No one is capable of more friendship than a dog. They spend their life waiting for any act of kindness. They spend their life waiting for the sound of your voice. You can tell that by the way they wag their tail.

They spend their life listening for your footsteps. Sometimes they can even recognize the sound your automobile makes. In return, all they ask for is some fresh water and a little food. Happiness for them is walking by your side. Ecstasy is the time you give them for play. They are anxious to do your bidding, and when they are no longer capable of these simple pleasures of life, they are content to die knowing that you took care of them and that they in return gave you friendship and love.

Etienne Dreyfous

Director general, Air France

A pterodactyl
to fly in the past
knowing the future.

The Earl of Dudley

Industrialist, peer

Fur

Does darling Fleur now have in mind,
Like Circe, to transform mankind?
And on her island filled with flowers,
Spellbind us with her artist's powers?
The smiles upon her tiger's face,
Do they recall the human race?
And will Fleur use her magic lore
To turn me into carnivore?
Since steak tartare's my special hate
I'd sooner choose another fate.
What animal resembles man?
Perhaps the great orangutan,
And if a man I cannot be
I'll settle for a mere monkey.
So, thanks to Fleur, when next you see
One in the zoo, it may be me.

Gerald Durrell

Author, chairman of the Jersey Wildlife Preservation Trust

꠸

At one time or another, everyone has had to go to one of those gigantic cocktail parties, to be bored mindless in the futile belief that you might find somebody interesting lurking in the sea of chattering jobbernowls. For my sins, I have been present at many such gatherings and find that there is only one thing to do and that is to regard the beehive of humanity as one would regard, say, a weaver bird colony, a flock of walrus, or a herd of bison, and compare their behavior. I call it Anthropomorphic Martini Research.

I was attending one of these faunistic gaggles consisting of publishers who thought they were contributing to literature, authors who *knew* they were, and critics who knew that, if only they were literate, they could be better than both authors and publishers. It was as deafening as a discotheque but slightly more inert. I was on my fifth drink, watching a little man with so much dandruff on his collar that he looked like a sort of carunculated miniature Mont Blanc (who was going through all the mating displays of a rock-hopper penguin with his pretty escort), when I suddenly became aware that I was myself observed.

Looking across the field of mopping and mowing humans, I saw that I was being scrutinized by a giraffe, a creature that I have always considered to be one of the most elegant beasts on earth. This giraffe, however, had been dressed by Christian Dior and was aglitter with earrings and bracelets. As I watched, fascinated, she slid across the room to my side with all the marvelous ease of the animal she so closely resembled. When she was nearer, I had to admire the eyes like dew-drenched black pansies; the long, beautifully shaped neck; the skin, that precise shade of coppery butter that can be applied only by the Mediterranean sun; the mane of dark hair; and the delicate nostrils on the alert for lions or other predators.

"Hello," she said, in a voice like a celestial viola. "What are you looking at so intently?"

"Madam," I said— seizing, with the skill acquired in this sort of gathering, a couple of drinks from a passing waiter— "Madam, I am at this moment looking at a giraffe which is infinitely more attractive than the rock-hopper penguin I was contemplating previously."

"Explain," she said, looking at me so seductively that I had to have a steadying drink of my martini.

"When you come to a party of this magnitude, with such a lava flow of bores, there is only one thing you can do if you want to preserve your sanity, and that is to indulge in Anthropomorphic Martini Research," I said.

"What has that got to do with giraffe?" she said.

"Well, you look like a giraffe," I said.

"I have *not* got spots," she pointed out.

"No," I agreed, "that is your only blemish."

She laughed. Giraffes are voiceless, but if they could laugh they would all have wanted to laugh like this.

"Let me show you how to play this game," I said. "Look, for example, at the gentleman with the dandruff. He is worried about his partner. He is not sure yet whether he has captured her devotion. Note the way he keeps pushing that ashtray toward her. Penguins do this with pebbles when they are courting. Look at the man over there with the face like a slab of fresh tunny. He is worried about that younger man invading his territory. See the way he is pawing the ground just like a buffalo, and moving round and round the girl."

"Fascinating," she said, musingly, her eyes like damp black velvet, "fascinating."

"Look," I said, "this is positively the most revolting party I have ever been to. Why don't we grab a couple more drinks and then I'll take you out to dinner?"

"I would love that," she said, sorrowfully, "but I don't think my husband would approve."

"Great heavens!" I said. "I am only inviting you out to *dinner*, not a weekend in Paris!"

"I know," she said, mournfully, "but there are other things to consider."

"What can possibly keep you riveted to this ghastly party?" I inquired.

"Well, I am the hostess," she said. . . .

When I am reincarnated, I am coming back as a male giraffe, in the hopes that I will have better luck next time.

Chief S. L. Edu

Founder and chairman, Nigerian Conservation Foundation

꒱

Given a choice, I would wish to be reincarnated as the rare and uniquely handsome antelope, called the greater kudu. Its characteristics appeal to me because some may unwittingly bear similarities to my own idiosyncrasies. They include shyness, harmlessness (except in self-defense), unobtrusiveness, grace, and magnificent presence—plus certain interesting features of its romantic behavior.

In romance, kudus are reputed to be very discreet in lovemaking (no one has yet succeeded in taking photographs in the wild of them mating). In captivity, however, one can observe the bull kudu demonstratively throwing his magnificent spiral (or rather corkscrew) horns on to his neck to pursue the fleeing female, and then laying his head on her back. After the ritual lovemaking, an exciting game follows when, running at full speed, the admirer tenderly rubs his cheek against the flank of the female, while making gentle clicking noises. He then pushes his neck across hers and the caress is enhanced by the soft waving of his mane. What a caring lover!

Being shy but individualistic creatures, kudus move in very small groups to form herds of not more than thirty. Extremely wary, these nocturnal activists hide by day in thickets or in the shade, away from predators and hunters, only coming out to graze late in the day, warning the rest of the herd and other animals nearby of threatening danger. Being herbivores, their eating habits are quite naturally clean as they feed mainly on shoots of trees, leaves, and fresh grass.

To the collector of trophies, whose hunting expeditions still require visible proof to impress friends at home, the evasive and cautious kudu offers the lesson that in the sport of hunting the gun be replaced with the camera—to compel the human race to protect and preserve what is left of these endangered species for the benefit of posterity. In the foregoing circumstances, I would cherish being such a creature if I were to be an animal in the next life.

Elizabeth Emanuel

Couturier

If I came back in a new life I would definitely choose to be a CAT.

To my minds CATS have the most PURRfect lifestyle imaginable—they spend the whole day lazing around on the best FURniture and eating food PURRchased specially for them, without a care in the world, and they don't know the meaning of the word CATastrophe. If they feel CLAWstro-phobic indoors they can always go out for a little sport (CATching birds perhaps), then PAWS to get their breath back. They are cosseted and pampered by their owners, and their lives do not enTAIL any hardship—in fact I would state CATegorically that no other animal is as relaxed as the CAT. If you give them a FURtive glance they merely gaze back at your serenely. Although CATS have no real PURRpose in life, for the ultimate luxurious existence you need look no FURther. Should you wish to find out more about the CAT, I will reFUR you to an excellent CATalog on the subject. But I must end here—there's a CLAWS in my contract that says this has to be WHISKERed off to the printers at once. . . .

Douglas Fairbanks, Jr.

Actor, writer, producer

I have given the question of what animal I would like to be, should reincarnation be "in the cards," such thought as could be spared. I imagine that too many people have already said that few things could be more happily anticipated than to come back as a dog in the British Isles. However, presuming that list is overbooked, I think my next choice would be to return as a tortoise in the Galapagos Islands. They are said to live to a wonderful old age; nobody bothers them very much; and they can prowl around and look at so many interesting things at their enviable leisure in the magnificent south Pacific climate.

Sensitive or emotional tortoises may envy some other more agile and energetic animals, but I should imagine, given the circumstances of their existence, they eventually become philosophical about it.

I would, however, add one condition which would be that I could retain some vestige of human awareness of my good fortune. How sad it would be to have all the lovely, lazy advantages and not consciously appreciate them. Other than that, the only *dis*advantage I can see is that, come spring and romance in the air, wooing must be damned difficult if not sometimes (but obviously not always) disheartening.

J. A. Floyd

Chairman, Christie's

I can think of no better fate than to return as a dog belonging to my wife!

Dame Margot Fonteyn
Prima ballerina, author, TV star

At first I thought I would choose to be a penguin because it would be wonderful not to feel the cold. Also they move with such style, look so elegant and so immaculately dressed, and apparently have a happy-go-lucky attitude to life—although I know appearances can be deceptive. The stumbling block is that I cannot stand raw fish and I understand they eat about thirty pounds a day each. So that's out.

Of course, one knows of many cats and dogs—ours for a start—who lead idyllic lives, but I couldn't risk being one of the millions who are starved, kicked, mangy, infested, intimidated, and totally unloved. Nor would I like the idea, even though it would hardly matter when I was dead, of being skinned for my cheap fur or sold for meat pies or whatever the local equivalent might be. It wouldn't be so bad to end up a fiddle string if it was in the hands of a good musician. Imagine contributing for years to the finest symphony concerts!

But there is also the risk of being an overspoiled pet kept indoors and stuffed exclusively with tinned foods—which are all right some of the time, but I do prefer fresh air and fresh foodstuffs.

The more I think about it the more I conclude that the most enviable and perfect animal is the koala bear. It has no enemies (now that humans are forbidden to capture or kill koalas); it hurts no other living creature; it eats only tasty young eucalyptus leaves; sleeps all day and plays around happily all night. Furthermore it is of an independent spirit and defies scientific efforts to discover its exact habits of living.

So I would choose to be a koala.

Bryan Forbes

Film producer, actor, writer

If I came back in a new life as an animal, my choice would be a domestic cat (though hopefully not as a neutered tom). As a personal choice I prefer cats to dogs, who always seem to me to have a somewhat slavish and sycophantic personality, whereas cats are much more self-possessed and grant favors only when it suits them. Based on the love and attention that my own various cats have had over the years, their style of life is most appealing, and I look forward to a second stay on earth being fed regularly and sleeping whenever the mood takes me. Not a very original choice, I grant you, but possibly due to the fact that I write this with my usual jet lag and would love to curl up somewhere—catlike—and sleep undisturbed.

The second part of your inquiry relates to whether I have an obsession to save a particular vanishing species, and in answer to this I can only say that I view with regret all and any species that are endangered and I feel that mankind has a great deal to answer for. I belong to many societies concerned with cruelty to animals and their preservation, and throughout my life I have always been attracted to a variety of species. As a child I formed a passionate attachment to a pig which I saved from the slaughterhouse and trained like a dog. It came when I whistled and allowed me to ride on its back. Although I have no wish to return as a pig, I do think they are a much maligned species and have very engaging personalities. If I may digress on Nanette's behalf, she is a positive Florence Nightingale where small rodents and birds are concerned. Many a time she has rescued the victims of our felines, nursed them, and sent them back into the world fortified by brandy. There must be whole colonies of mice inhabiting our garden who have a pronounced liking for alcoholic beverages!

Eileen Ford

Director, Ford Model Agency

I am afraid that if I came back to life as an animal, it wouldn't be because I liked the animal so much, but because, it seems to me, that the animal has rather got the best of it.

I think it would be as a Black Angus breeding bull for the reason that they are very well fed, are groomed every day, and seem to have nothing to do but produce offspring without any of the fuss that the poor cow must endure. A breeding bull is never turned into a Black Angus steak, and it seems to me to lead a very cushy life.

I like cats the best of any animal, then dogs and other strays there might be. When I retire, it is my hope to have a home for waifs, including those poor wild horses who suffer such fearful fates.

Clare Francis

Round-the-world solo sailor, author

Since I am a vegetarian I think I would have to choose a herbivorous animal, and the one that immediately springs to mind is a gorilla. Although represented as an aggressive animal, the gorilla is really a big baby who is very loyal to its group and to its family. I also suspect that gorillas have a lot of fun, and it seems a pity to come back in another life and be bored. The gorilla is not, of course, very graceful or beautiful, but I do not think that matters because, hopefully, one would be beautiful to other gorillas. Also, gorillas are in need of protection as an endangered species, and so I think the more of us who come back in the next life as gorillas, the better.

Sir Vivian Fuchs

Explorer, former president
Royal Geographic Society

When I was a boy I was always busy with some outdoor project, preferably by water or in the forest. I could dam a stream and learned to fell trees—which I still do. I think therefore that I must choose to come back as a beaver, for they too inhabit rivers and forests, and are endlessly busy.

They are also ingenious, work hard at cutting down trees and building dams to make pools where they can build their "lodges." In summer the water protects them from wolves and other enemies. When winter comes the pool freezes over, but the water below affords access to the "lodge" which, being constructed of wood and mud, becomes a frozen fortress—impregnable to marauding predators prowling over the ice.

I think I could feel very comfortable as a beaver, IF ONLY MEN WOULD LEAVE ME ALONE TO ENJOY LIFE.

The Life of the Beaver

Oh! I'm a clever beaver with a long and flattened tail,
I seldom leave the river, where I use it as a flail,
To drive me through the water where the currents never fail.
With webs to aid progression and claws to keep possession
I build my dams and lodges without a single lesson.

Who else can deepen rivers to keep the ice at bay
And build their homes of trees and stones and frozen mud
and clay?
Yes, I'm a clever beaver who works from night to day.
For I feed on vegetation and gnaw the trunks of trees
Till they tumble in the river with the smallest little breeze.

Once we populated rivers throughout the frozen north,
But now that Man has found us we dare not sally forth.
For all that he can think of is what our skins are worth,
Cannot someone speak for us and offer some affection?
For all we ask of humankind is just the Law's protection.

If only I was human for just a single day
I'd solve the pressing problem in quite a simple way.
For every skin they took from us they'd surely have to pay
With one month's solo sojourn in the river's winter water,
Without the aid of clothes and fires, or even bricks
and mortar.

Nicholas Gage

Author, producer

If I were to come back an animal, I suspect it would be as a lion.

I didn't know my birthdate until I was in my twenties, when an old woman from my village told me I was born on July 23—the cusp of Leo.

All my life I have been told I look and behave like a Leo, with a large leonine head and mane of hair.

I have a temper that flares quickly, but, as friends and family have learned, I roar for a moment and then the storm is over.

Leos are supposed to be happiest when telling others what to do, loyal and fierce in defending their own, protective of their own turf and family—all of this, I am told, describes me.

If the analogy ran true all the way, I suppose I should be working for MGM's lion, instead of Paramount, whose symbol is a mountain. Come to think of it, I was born in the mountains of northern Greece, so perhaps I should come back as a mountain goat—they're plentiful in my native province of Epiros. But who would choose to be a mountain goat when he could come back as the King of Beasts instead?

Jane Gaskell

Novelist, astrologist

⊃✕

Little snake, little quick shrewd snake, perhaps brown.

Little snake that melds in with the jungle it flickers through, becoming now a tree root, now a liana. Little snake always camouflaged, until it decides to appear from nowhere, menacing enough to make at least some predators think again.

Little quick snake that never has trouble with the tax man, the home-extension builders who waltz rings around the home extender, the scaffolders, the loud kids with the kitten-killing Alsatian across the street.

No, no trouble with the tax man nor with the tumble-drier man who says he doesn't have the spare part and he'll call again with it in ten days if ever. On the contrary, the little snake lies dreaming in the flowers on the high creeper in the sun, living really on their fragrance, eating infrequently and then dreaming off the meal again, so that dreams double for digestion.

The little snake is infinitely flexible, ready at any given moment to go this way or that, at just minimal notice. The little snake, its ear to the ground, hears the jungle's messages almost before they are sent out; interprets them and without shilly-shally, without having to telephone friends or accountants or solicitors for advice, knows which way to bend.

The snake can flick out of a tight corner, a matter of inching through a keyhole, disappearing through a loophole.

The snake can give others a foothold on the seemingly sheer rock face, presenting itself as a handy stirrup shape.

The snake is a tempter: ready to pull a skein of golden glimmer across a gray situation. The snake can deliver the goods, too. The temptations outside the Garden were not all hollow promises. There is a freedom in standing on your own ground. The snake can even cross bridges that have already been burned, with a back flip and somersault and a bit of a toss of the head.

Charles De Haes

Director general, World Wildlife Fund

As a leader of a conservation organization and a defender of wildlife in all its variety, I have thought seriously about my answer to your question as to what animal I would like to be in the hereafter.

My work, and therefore my present existence, is closely linked to the creatures with which man shares the earth. Alas, the future of so many animals and their wild habitats is so threatened by man's mismanagement of the environment that the prospect of becoming an endangered species in my next life is hardly appealing. Anyone who believes in reincarnation should be a dedicated conservationist.

My choice is to be an elephant, and here are my reasons.

The elephant is the most powerful of all animals and fears no other. Yet it does not abuse its power. It is gentle and threatens no one. It lives in and for its family and its group. Those who have seen elephants trying to revive a fallen comrade know that elephants feel compassion and are loyal.

In an age where insecurity is rife and moral standards decline, the elephant stands firm and is a symbol of nobility and peace. The elephant is a survivor; it will dig for water and find it in a desert and lead its family long distances to food. When threatened by its only enemy, man, it does not run away, but will charge, trumpeting. It also trumpets for pleasure and for love.

The elephant eats up to 400 kg of its favorite food every day and doesn't put on excess fat. Now that's an attribute to envy.

Yes, I would like to be an elephant. But, since reincarnation may be going on all the time, perhaps I have been one already and my subconscious is calling me to return.

Sir Peter Hall

Director, National Theatre, London

Having just directed sheep, hens, cows, pigs, dogs, chickens, rats, pigeons, ducks, a cat, etc., etc., in my adaption of *Animal Farm* I don't want to come back another sort of animal.

Olivia De Havilland

Actress, author, lecturer

In October 1967, after the New York premiere of the 70mm presentation of *Gone with the Wind*, the great trial lawyer Louis Nizer and his charming wife, together with Jack Valenti, president of the Motion Pictures Association, took me to supper at 21.

Instructing me to reply instantly and without thought, Louis asked me the following questions: "If you could be a bird, which one would you choose to be?" I heard myself say, "A dove." "If you could be an animal, which one would you be?" At once I said, "A gazelle."

Louis then commented, "Ah! No capacity for self-defense!"

He thereupon turned to Jack Valenti and posed the same questions. To the first Jack answered, "An eagle"; to the second, "A black panther."

Since Jack is a Texan, it is not surprising that he chose the king of the skies and the king of the forest and veld as the creatures he would like to be—both eminently capable of defending themselves should any beast or bird be witless enough to threaten them.

What was extraordinary was that there we were: Jack and I, seated side by side—he my natural enemy, I his natural victim. Heaven knows what might have happened if the food at 21 had not been exceptionally copious and delectable that evening.

As to Louis, when (even though I may be a dove) I turned the tables by asking him the very same question he had asked of us—he said, "A rooster and a poodle."

Both are show creatures: the first aggressive and the ruler of the roost; the second intelligent, nimble, and inescapably the center of attention. No wonder Louis Nizer always wins in court.

Dr. John Hemming

Director, Royal Geographic Society

My choice of animal reincarnation would be a coati (*nasua narica*), a furry little creature that roams in the Amazon forests. Coatis are mischievous, fearless, and very curious. They have long, sensitive noses that they poke into everything in their search for grubs or eggs. They are convivial, moving about in packs of ten to twenty, and one that I had briefly as a pet seemed to have a delightful sense of humor. It saw the joke in disrupting papers on my desk, and loved to hang on to the outside of a jeep with the wind on its whiskers. The attraction of being a coati is to live in the beautiful cool rain forests, running up the trees and far out on to their branches. Coatis have few enemies. But if cornered in a tree they roll themselves into balls—to protect those delicate noses—and drop to the ground. I do not know whether this is my character. Probably not. But it is good to think of being a carefree, busy, and quite intelligent little creature at large in the jungle.

David Hicks

Interior designer, author

If I were to come back in a new life as an animal I would choose to be a unicorn because they are so elegant and romantic. Essentially masculine but whimsical, decorative but protective, one would support the arms of endless sovereigns, perch aloft on state occasions, and pose over select butchers' and grocers' windows and be stamped on the cover of passports traveling the world.

I would nestle in the folds of Mortlake tapestries, gallop through Dali landscapes, and being legendary and chivalrous I would not need to complain or explain. It would be pleasing to know that my single horn was unique.

Nancy Holmes

Author, publicist

It—a very small and built-for-action package of black spots on white—came tearing around a corner of the small English farm, deep in the springtime greenery of Devon countryside. Warm eyes gleaming, it introduced itself to the visitors, as if to say, "Hello, hello, it's me, and who are you?"

Dazzled by this small beast, I said to the ample farm lady, "What is *that*?"

Grabbing it up in her arms, she replied, "She's a Jack Russell terrier."

Without a moment's hesitation, I heard myself asking, "Is she for sale?"

"Of course," the farm lady said, looking at me as if I were daft. "I'll take a fiver for her."

To my astonishment, I took a five-pound note out of my bag and gave it to her. The deal was done. It was the best transaction I ever made.

Her name immediately became Jane Russell, due to the sly sophistication of the writer David Rook who had brought me to that pleasant farm on that lovely day. Jack Russell terriers are rare creatures—dogs, if you insist—and Miss Jane Russell had every quality I had always admired and often faked. She was courageous to the point of insanity, calm to a degree of true wisdom, and more fun than anyone I have ever known. She was devious if need be and truly clever in her own spirited way. She knew when to go away and she knew when to come back. She traveled well and never complained that I took her away from her natural fox-hunting habitat.

She got her way in matters of importance, she was full of surprises, and she was nobody's fool. She knew how to behave and how to flirt, and she had a thousand fans at least.

Omar Sharif loved her once in Greece, when, during the course of a film being made there, he informed the Greek press that world-famous Jane Russell was also staying in his hotel. Omar told them that she was at the very moment by the pool sunning herself. My Jane Russell was, in fact, playing soccer with the pool attendant. The press never found her, and Omar and Jane laughed for weeks. The stars of *Hair,* who had once taken care of her in California during the days when I was working and they were not, recognized her walking on the street with me in New York. "Janie!" they yelled, with glee. She leaped into Berger's arms, plastering the star with fervent kisses. The whole lot of them ignored me, her friend and somewhat owner, completely.

She's been gone for some time now. I'm still here, but if I ever come back, I'd like to come back with her. Or *be* her.

Roger Horchow

Horchow Collection

I have decided that I would like to come back, if given the privilege, as a dachshund. A dachshund is a smart animal but small enough to be allowed to stay inside a good deal. They seem to have subtle senses of humor, and the kinds of people they live with strike me as being generally interesting, kind, and affectionate. All of that would suit me just fine, and I would hope to have a long and happy life with my new owner in my new life.

Thomas Hoving

Editor-in-chief, *Connoisseur* magazine

I would love to be an otter. No creature I know of happens to pack so much beauty, strength, athletic ability, grace, cunning, speed, agility, intelligence, and familial concern into such a small, gorgeous frame. One special trait of the creatures is their obsession for play (which at times can be a bit too wild and all-consuming). I don't really know what otters think about the Italian Renaissance or the Wilton diptych or the Ghent altarpiece or the works of Pablo Picasso in the divine years 1926–1928, or Donatello and Bramante or the watercolors of Blake or the illustrations of Hokusai or the Arena Chapel and the Sistine ceiling and the Bury St. Edmunds cross or the Limbourg brothers. But if I became an otter, I'd teach my friends that this stuff is worthy of their bright attention. I bet they would agree.

With warm regards, from the hope-to-be otter.

Gayle Hunnicut

Actress

I would wish to live my life as an eagle, soaring above the great and grand landscapes of the world; living in solitary splendor with independence of heat and fierceness of spirit. But I fear that this is only the idealized hope of a domesticated marmalade cat, destined to remain peacefully at home.

Vane Ivanović

Consul general for
Great Britain in Monaco

The challenge here posed is founded on the fancy of reincarnation. On this premise I would have all the time in this world to decide the final incarnation in which to take my place in the queue on Judgment Day. What form of life then to choose for my first "comeback"? A bacterium.

It is no exaggeration to say that upon the activities of bacteria the very existence of man depends. Nor could there be any other living thing in the world without bacteria. Every animal and plant owes its existence to the fertility of the soil, and this in turn depends on the activity of microorganisms that inhabit the soil in almost inconceivable numbers.

Bacteria have been around much longer than any other living entity. They undergo variations without fuss. They have proved wise and competent enough to survive all the changes of conditions that have taken place on earth. They even avoided extinction during the legendary flood that wiped out almost everything else. Such a magnificent capacity to survive and go on reproducing demonstrates that bacteria possess greater and more thorough knowledge of life on earth than other beings.

A millenium or so as sturdy bacterium might also provide me with a chance to learn about the desire for power; how to select the means of its exercise, how to use it and not to abuse it. I would have a new insight into problems of the individual and a glimpse at an ancient community life in the hope of acquiring better understanding of ethics and morals.

If I came back as a bacterium on my very first reincarnation I would be better equipped to enjoy subsequent and less exacting lives in forms more in accord with my present taste— the superbly elegant shark, the self-sufficient eagle, the patient tortoise, or the brave Iberian bull. In time, I might even be blessed with sufficient grace to acquire the faith and courage necessary to face the final day as a man once more.

Beverley Jackson

Socialite, columnist

If I had one bit of common sense, my choice would be to return as one of my own dogs. What a fabulous life they enjoy in beautiful Santa Barbara, California! Suppers of chicken breast, runs on the beach, bedded in a king-sized bed beneath the finest linen sheets, which they reluctantly share with me.

Tempting as this all is, I confess that life in the Far Eastern jungle calls to me. Yes, my choice is to come back as a great massive bundle of black and white fluffy fur—to spend my next life romping through the rain forests of China, chomping away on bamboo. And of course this life would still offer me the opportunity for travel since the leaders of China are now most generous in sending a panda or two off for temporary residence in foreign lands. It is definitely the panda bear's life for me on my second time around. . . .

David Jacobs

TV and radio personality

It has taken me quite a long time to decide what animal I would like to be on my return visit to this earth, but I have decided quite unequivocally that if I come back at all, and I believe I will, it will be as a large, powerful, ferocious, arboreal, anthropoid ape.

On my current visit I have spent the majority of my years as a total physical coward more able to deal with heavy emotional crises, so I suppose you can't have everything, but if at any time danger has lurked in the form of a physical fight my knees have always turned to water and my feet to jelly. I really would like also to not have to appear to be quite as smooth as I am accused of being. So, let me swing from the trees, roar ferociously, and be second to none. To have people running away from me in terrified disorder and disarray would thrill me; in fact to coin a phrase, I'd "go ape."

Mrs. Lyndon B. Johnson

Former First Lady

If I were to choose the animal for my "re-incarnation," it would probably be a cat. A cat is something of an enigma and they amuse me. You always know where you stand with a dog, but never with a cat! They are the most self-contained animals I have observed and the most ingratiating. I love the way they rub affectionately against the leg—but wonder if they are sincere and needful—and that contented sound of purring. But mainly, a cat is highly independent and always lands on its feet! It enjoys the good things of life, but survives the hardest knocks.

Another animal I regard with sheer delight and may want to "come back" as is the giraffe. They are so stately and regal and survey the world around them from that height with a gentle assured air. Besides, for once I would be slim enough (did you ever see a fat giraffe?)!!

Melanie Kahane

Industrial and interior designer

I have often tried to adjust my fantasies to a potential "hereafter" with a rationale that would project some realistic results.

If indeed reincarnation is a fallout of this present sequence, then who was I "before"? Who will I "return" as? Since you offer me a choice for the latter (and I admit—it is the only offer of reincarnation I've had) and you already have me assigned to the animal world, then I want to be an elegant cheetah. I think, instinctively, as a female, I relate to felines. I like their independent style, their deceptive strength and still their need for a society—a social order.

Among all animal species I would prefer to be a cheetah, to be endowed with their exquisite grace of movement, their unchallenged speed, their confident sureness and unique dress of rich elegant colors.

They are hardly the largest in the kingdom, nor do they traditionally hold titles, but they are noble. Within their laws they are just. I like that.

I have one reservation: Since cheetahs all look so much alike I should prefer to be somewhat distinctive—different. Unless, of course, all of us look alike to cheetahs.

I should also choose a gregarious group if this could be arranged. I have never understood why they are so socially incestuous. Don't they ever visit with that nice Tiger family or consort with those aristocratic Lions—whom do their children play with? Don't they ever intermarry? Are they all indigenous racists?

I might have second thoughts about this. . . .

Deborah Kerr

Actress

🙰

I think if I came back to this world (which at the *moment* is a grim prospect!), I would love to be a bird called a hoopoe; a bird that is eminently paintable! We have many here in our hideaway in Spain, and I adore to watch them digging up worms, or whatever, with their long elegant, curved beaks, on the lawn right in front of the house. If you have a bird book, you will see how decorative they are, with their boldly barred black and white wings and tail, pinkish-brown plumage on the body, and the eternally amusing and beautiful crest—rust-colored and tipped with black—on their heads, which they raise on landing. Their voice is a low and far-carrying *"Poo poo poo"*—always three notes! They are so fascinating to watch, and as we have a family that returns every spring to nest in the Spanish oak behind the house, I feel as if they are friends! They are so exotic and unusual—perhaps this is indicative of a deeply hidden desire in me to be exotic and unusual!

Karl Lagerfeld

Couturier

What would you choose to be if you came back in a new life as an animal? *A dachshund*. And why? They seem to have a greater sense of humor than all the other animals.

Eleanor Lambert

Publicist

I would like to be reincarnated as a miniature Italian greyhound or whippet. Both of these sleek, pretty animals are a lot of things I'm not but wish I were: willowy, thin, petted, always decorative, single-minded. The only traits we share are brown eyes and loads of nervous energy.

My next choice would be to be a hummingbird. I named my Acapulco house Tzinzunzan (Aztec for hummingbird), and with all the traveling I do, I must be halfway into that state of being by now.

Dominique Lapierre

Author

⤝

I want to be reincarnated into a migrative bird. Possibly a flamingo. A few reasons:

1. I have always been fascinated with the flexibility of living into *(sic)* another dimension than the *plancher des vaches* as we say in French. This idea of flying over the earth is quasi-mystical for me.
2. My whole life has been migrative, from one place to another. The idea is to continue to do this with my sole energy, without a passport, visas, or currency controls, etc. . . .
3. A flamingo has no enemies.
4. A flamingo nests only in warm places. I hate the cold, the snow, winter sports, etc. . . . My *querencia* is a hot sanded beach, palm trees, smells of *bazari*, exotic cities. The Orient.

Richard E. Leakey

Anthropologist, author

Given the choice for a second existence I would almost certainly opt to be an African Batleur eagle although in ab-
stract, my choice for a once-only existence would have been
to be exactly myself.

The attraction that I see in the life of this African eagle is
that the Batleur has tremendous grace; it spends most of its
time in easy soaring flight, riding the exciting thermal air
currents. It is comfortable in a variety of African environs
ranging from the deserts to the mountains, and because of
its keen eyesight and powerful build, it is seldom short of
food. The bird has a long life, is seldom afflicted by disease,

and like others of its kind, enjoys a perfect family life. The courtship is fierce, the bonding secure, the ties are affectionate, and once the young are reared, they leave the nest and are gone forever.

Most eagles are handsome and proud, but the Batleur is perhaps among the most striking. The bright-red bill, the contrasting black and white feathers, and the cut of the wing in flight guarantee that it is distinctive among the distinctive! That sort of existence cannot be bad.

Bernard Levin

Author, critic, columnist

A cat, of course! And it won't be the first time—I have been a cat in several earlier incarnations. It's not just that they live high on the hog (though they do), but because of their grace, their independence, their wary affections, and above all their mystery. This may well be the mystery of the universe—at any rate it is a secret of tremendous importance to us as well as them, *and they won't tell.* So the only way I am ever to penetrate the secret is to become one myself.

John V. Lindsay

Attorney, former
mayor of New York City

I've always liked the eagle, because I'm a mountain man—
as well as an ocean man—and go to high places. Mary and
I own some land on top of a mountain in the Rocky Mountains. We look for eagles. We just came back from Nepal
where we were camping for a couple of weeks at the foot of
the Himalayas. Saw some eagles.

The bald eagle is particularly American and I relate to
that. But all eagles fight not to become extinct. Like so many
earthly creatures they are an endangered species.

I've always found that the higher I get above the ground,
the better the place looks.

Mrs. James Paul Linn

Hostess

But why would anyone want to come back?
Except to escape a hell-fired state,
And then to atone for previous lack
Of creature love, thereby seeking new fate.
Yet for Fleur's fantasy, back I will come
As a Lhasa bitch who has but one eye
And a fearsome look purported by some
To proclaim: Queen; while others, who may lie,
Offer another view: of actions bold,
Of efforts many, energy to burn
In being a Lady of whom its told,
In truth, gives love and is loved in return.
Doobie is my name, happy as can be
Knowing my mistress would want to be me.

Moira Lister

Actress

Of course all the luxurious animals spring to mind like the voluptuous Russian sable or lynx or snow leopard—but I would have to remember I would be an endangered species—life a constant awareness of traps and guns and man bent on destruction and gain.

So my mind wandered to less spectacular animals; being an actress, I settled for a chameleon! I would have a head like a helmet to protect me from the blows that rain from our modern sky. I would be physically equipped for arboreal life, living in leafy glades where the sun dapples through just enough to warm to a luxuriant lethargy.

Food would be no problem, as my feet and hands would be neatly arranged as grasping organs. I would easily get to the top of trees, where "the higher up, the sweeter it grows"—and just hang in there, waiting for a succulent morsel to pass by. My unique tongue would flick out to an alarming length and lunch would be served!

My fascinating eyes would move independently, lulling my prey into a false security, until the second I decide upon the victim. With the speed of light, they'd then focus together. It is said no earthly creature can resist the honing in of that enveloping spell.

The greatest game would be to change color and sink into nature's camouflage—like leaf or bark or indeed man's Savile Row suit. Then I would have the most fun. On a hot summer's day, I could perch on a friend's shoulder, listen to his deepest secrets (unobserved by most and hypnotizing others).

At night, I'd snuggle up on his pillow and go to sleep dreaming of all my aspirational changes. If I could change not only my color but my shape (like the frog), I'd become a prince—or play all those characters that people my theatrical canvas.

I think if I showed this analogy to a psychiatrist he or she would come up with some very pertinent deductions!

Lady Elizabeth Longford

Author

᠍᠍᠊᠍᠊

I suppose a true animal-lover would prefer to be any animal rather than a human being. I always remember Walt Whitman's praise of animals:

They do not sweat and whine about their condition,
They do not lie awake in the dark and weep for their
    sins . . .
Not one is dissatisfied, not one demented with the mania of
  owning things,
Not one kneels to another . . .
Not one is respectable or unhappy over the whole earth.

If they were really all as perfect as Whitman says I should find it extremely hard to choose one species from among so many for my transmigration. But of course Whitman was wrong. Not all dogs refrain from whining or passionately owning a decayed bone buried in my garden. Spaniels cringe, their form of kneeling, and pedigree dogs are immensely respectable. The cows in a neighbor's field lie awake at night mooing, and for all I know they are weeping for their sins.

The only animal I know that neither sweats, whines, weeps, kneels, is respectable or unhappy is the cat. And this is what I would choose to be. A stray cat. In Sussex we call stray cats "Metty" because they are met-up-with. My Metty was very affectionate and never "walked by herself," as Kipling mistakenly said, except when she walked over the fields to join our family. She chose us, and now I choose her. She had short thick black fur, yellow eyes, and a sinuous relaxed body that lasted in perfection for fourteen years, until one morning she quietly but firmly refused to be "put out" and at the end of the day died curled up on her chair.

To be honest, I have one doubt about being a cat. Cats don't like water and I particularly love the sea. Perhaps after all I ought to take this chance of being a water animal. Suddenly, as I wonder which water animal and ponder over the very deserving coelacanth which is nearly but not quite extinct, I have an inspiration. Surely there must be such a thing as a sea cat? After all there are sea horses, sea cows, sea dogs, sea urchins. I lug out my huge single-volume *Shorter Oxford English Dictionary* from the bookshelf and turn to "sea." Oh joy, there's an endless stream of sea things. I can't believe that "sea cat" is not among them.

I dash through all the listed animals: sea fox (hippo), sea bear (fur seal), sea canary (white whale), sea hawk (skua), sea goose (phalarope), sea coot (cormorant), and many other sea birds; sea adder (pipe fish), sea angel and lots of other sea fish; sea hare (mollusc), sea hog (porpoise), sea pheasant (turbot), sea toad (fishing frog), sea unicorn (narwhal), sea calf (common seal), sea devil (stingray), sea elephant, sea wife, sea god, sea dragon, and so on and so forth for four whole columns. But believe it or not there is no sea cat among them.

So it is a choice for me between cat and water. Cat it will be. For I have just thought of one extra reason for being a cat. Cats are among the most popular of all animals; *vide* the ancient Egyptians, T. S. Eliot, A. L. Rowse, *et al*. Therefore Fleur Cowles will be illustrating *Cats,* and I long to be drawn by Fleur Cowles. Her flower drawings are exquisite, so now I can enjoy not only her pictures of catmint *(nepeta cataria),* catkins (unisexual inflorescence), cat's-eye (germander speedwell), cat's-foot (ground ivy), cat's-tail (reed mace), and so on for two whole pages of my dictionary, but also her portrait of the one and indivisible Cathead itself. *Felis domesticus*. Meow. (My dictionary gives the first Meow in 1634. What did cats say before that? I shall find out when I become one.)

Shirley Lord

Editor, British *Vogue*

I thought a gnu would be new, but nobody knew what a gnu could do . . . so giving the question more serious thought (and deciding to avoid the trap of being original at all costs) I was torn between Paul Newman's cat—sleek gray and independent like its owner (and regularly stroked by those strong masculine hands)—and Nancy Kissinger's labrador retriever, Tyler, a personality in its own right, privy to so many fascinating conversations. A sofa was reserved for Tyler at the last Humane Society Benefit in New York. As a girl who graduated from the "University of Fleet Street" I know I would miss my byline and Tyler does get press mentions from time to time. Somehow it still wasn't right. Having a strong crush on everything Australian at the moment I mused on the idea of "coming back" as a koala bear—but in the end—after one week's deliberation—I realized I had no choice. To "come back" without the sea as part of my natural habitat would be agonizing, so perhaps in common with many of your friends I would choose to "return" as that most magical of creatures, a dolphin.

The Hon.
Clare Boothe Luce

Author, playwright,
U.S. ambassador to Italy, 1953–57

What animal would I choose if I were magically transformed into a lower life form? I have only one choice—a dolphin—the most adorable animal ever created on land or sea and the most intelligent.

Viscount Macmillan of Ovenden

Publisher

As far as I am concerned, I am not sure if I want to come back as an animal—probably as a mosquito *inside* an enemy's mosquito net!

As to what sort of animal I feel I *shall* come back as: why, one of Landseer's lions in Trafalgar Square. With pretensions to nobility, much "climbed on," but in the end only a target! Only to be saluted by the pigeons!

Mary Martin

Actress, songstress

I would choose to return as a poodle—all because of my darling Jerry! . . .

I, of course, have had Jerry with me as a newborn puppy and she is such a little lady—when you take her out for her walk—or even to put her in the car—she stops and twirls before going out the door—and does the same thing when she comes back in the door—she does this also many times during the day—she stops to let you in the door first—she is so intelligent and remembers residences once she has been there—when she goes to do her little "business" she turns her back and looks at you as much as to say, "Don't watch"—she will not perform if you are watching her—she never begs for food—never makes noise of any kind except when the doorbell rings and then she is a little "watchdog"—she is a miniature—white—but I do not dress her up in buttons and bows—and she loves *everybody*—she does not know a stranger when it comes to their wanting to hold her or pet her—she *loves* being loved—she has never played with the customary toys of a dog—but when I travel she remains with my secretary and loves to sit and sleep with her head in the lap of her (secretary's) stuffed bear—a darling sight! And when I return she greets me with squeals of delight and movement of her little body.

Georges Mathieu

Action painter

᠊ᢞ

Oh! What joy to have the opportunity at last to say what's in my heart, to bare my soul, and to set free my most secret thoughts, my wildest dreams. . . .

All right, yes, I'll tell you now; I would wish, in another life, to be a flea! This of course applies to the human flea, the *pulex irritans.*

Wouldn't it be wonderful to travel in enormous leaps at least a hundred times bigger than oneself, to vanish from the world by hiding in all kinds of places, to choose a cosy abode, to delight in the free, delicious nourishment of human blood, all the while giving the docile prey a thousand irritations, making her jump each time she feels an itch, a pinch, or a bite, each of which is accompanied by a glorious telltale yell revealing the effectiveness of the treatment. And what marvelous confirmation, a few moments later, are those magnificent eruptions of purple and red!

Also, what lovely excursions into the most picturesque areas: of wool, and cotton certainly, but also silk, lace, and lycra . . . landscapes of extreme softness, laid bare, deserted, sometimes even shaved, unknown scenes or glistening ones, long plains, dunes, mountains, forests, arbors, bushes, mysterious thickets, but also lakes, craters, precipices! All this without any formalities, any customs, or any passports . . .

Oh! to snuggle into sumptuous linen or satin sheets, expanses as intoxicating as the Russian steppes, surging over domes that have been bronzed in the burning sun. To choose beautiful, lithe victims and cover them with pustules, and then try to hide in a corner during their contortions, before escaping by fleeing from one to another; occasionally risking death, but a divine death between two varnished fingernails, drowning in one's own blood!

José Mayorga

Conservationist, philanthropist

I am really grateful for the kind invitation to become an animal, because it has helped me to discover my real self.

Comparing my conscience with natural instinct and human comfort with animal response to adversity, I will no longer exaggerate my little skills nor hide my weaknesses, and that will have made me a better person in case I am not successful in turning into an animal stronger and better endowed than I am now.

I prepared to lose my highly developed senses of taste and touch if I regain in full those of seeing, smelling, and hearing as well by night as by day. I want to be physically much stronger; stronger than any other animal.

As the mark of my station, I need to be clothed majestically with great beauty as a king recognized and respected by all the animals in my domains.

I will bring up my children in my own image as all my ancestors have done since the beginning of time, creating a tradition of conservative custom and manners which should be the envy of the erratic human species I am about to leave if I have the luck to become the only animal I would consider in my stead—a tiger.

Ian McCallum

Director, American Museum
at Bath, England

꒳

A rat. Why?

a) Intelligence—people are so hurtful in their remarks about unintelligent animals, but it is agreed that a rat is nothing if not intelligent.

b) Push—I do think if you are an animal you have to be pushy, especially with regard to feeding yourself—some go really too far, even indulging in cruelty, *viz.* cats. Rats, on the other hand, grab what they can get, without inordinate cruelty and without having to say "thank you" and seem to do pretty well at it.

c) Wanderlust—rats get around. Many other animals seem to be either house- or territory-bound, but rats have found, with extraordinary ingenuity, many, almost people-less, routes of travel. The sewers of the great cities of the world might have been designed for animals with wanderlust.

d) Spying—for a rat who wants a rest from long journeys, most houses provide all sorts of holes and crevices where the rat can enter for food, or bide its time while listening in to the not always boring gossip and antics of the human race.

e) Survival—rats seem in little danger of becoming a vanishing species. They need not, therefore, spend sleepless nights worrying about all those worthy humans spending sleepless nights devising fund-raising endeavors to save them.

Given their character and habitats there is a very good chance they will survive when the human species vanishes, an aim to which humans are devoting vast ingenuity and resources.

Lady McIndoe

Friend of the author

A bookworm: It will be my pleasure to eat other people's words rather than my own!

Virginia McKenna

Actress, animal protector

I know I'd love to be a bird—a lot of my dreams are concerned with flying. I flap my arms and soar above the tree tops! I love lions, butterflies, ladybirds, giraffe—I love all animals.

But I think there are more dimensions to the question than the emotional and aesthetic aspects—which are rather succinctly summed up by a poem our eldest son wrote while he was still at school. It is called "Wish":

Wish I was a fish
or maybe not
For if I was a fish I'd lie in stagnant pools
And rot.
Wish I was a bird
Who with boundless grace could fly and touch the sun
If I could see it through the fog—
The endless wreaths of aerodynamic smog.
Wish I was a stag
And could wander as I please
Through the forests of my realm
If forests there be, when concrete pillars
Supplement the tree—
What wish I?

So there would be no point in choosing the animal with the most chance of survival. In another life, I would choose the animal that embodied characteristics that are important to me; in which the family bond was strong and enduring; who cared for the old, the young and the sick. An animal who, in order to survive, caused the death of no other creature— eating leaves, grasses, twigs, and fruit. My animal has to be the elephant, that gentle giant who has tolerated and suffered in so many ways, at the hands of man. I love the elephant. I admire and respect its wise and kind nature. And I would consider it a great honor to be born again in its likeness.

Ed McMahon

Co-host, *The Tonight Show*

If I were an animal there's no doubt in my mind that I'd like to be a racehorse. You're well taken care of—groomed meticulously with lots of warm baths and rubdowns. Your main requirement is to run like the dickens for a couple of minutes several times in your life for which you are rewarded with beautiful roses to wear around your neck and dozens of pats on the back. Ah, but then comes the sweetest reward. After several years of being lauded as the greatest runner of all time you are then put into a field with lots of lovely ladies and the rest of your life to prove you are the greatest lover.

Lady Sonia Melchett

Board member, National Theatre, London

꒰꒰

Once, in Canada, I flew in a seaplane with a party of hunters to a place called Cabbage Willow Camp, north of Hudson Bay, in search of wild geese. These Canada and snow geese migrate from their Arctic nesting grounds in tens of thousands in the autumn and stay on the marshes at Hudson Bay to fatten up before their long flight south down the Mississippi valley to the southern states to spend the winter. I had never shot anything before and, in Montreal, learned with difficulty to use a shotgun.

We stayed at a camp consisting of two cabins—one, the cook's house, and the other the sleeping quarters for the hunters. Scattered around were a few tents for the local Cree Indian guides and their families. As the only woman in the party I was put in the cookhouse.

At four the next morning, while it was still dark, the Indians took us in canoes through the marshes to catch the early-morning flight from the sea. They built circular hides with cabbage-willow branches and then sculpted pieces of hard mud into which they stuck white feathers, arranging them in groups as if they were birds feeding on the marshes.

After a while we heard the extraordinary noise that a flock of geese makes in flight—rather like a lot of chattering women—but not a goose in sight. It was, in fact, the Indians lying among the decoys calling in the geese in a brilliant imitation of their own language. Soon, a flock of geese was flying in perfect formation across the gray sky, swooping down toward us. I dug my rifle into my armpit and, as I heard the shots around me, my fingers became paralyzed and I watched several proud and beautiful birds crash to the ground. The guides then made a different sound—the cry of a wounded goose. The depleted flock hesitated, turned, and once again flew across our hide, swooping down toward their wounded brethren. As the shots rang out I vowed I would never go shooting again.

But I would choose to come back in a new life as a wild goose. To me it evokes so many things I love and admire—beauty in motion, the sky in all its different moods—compassion for one's fellow creatures—the ability to travel great distances and see other countries without machines—the companionship of others. Above all I might discover the mystery of migration and what secret these birds possess that enables them to leave and arrive at precisely the same spot and time each year. Yes, I would like to be a wild goose.

> My heart knows what the wild goose knows
> And I must go where the wild goose goes
> Wild goose, brother goose, which is best—
> A wandering foot or a heart at rest?

Sir Yehudi Menuhin

Musician

Is it because I spend roughly one quarter of my year in airplanes, viewing the land stretched out below me, the sea an infinity of gray-blue, the mountains a glorious panorama of row upon row of miraculous white peaks; that in one single glimpse mine is the privilege of an omniscient sight tantamount to that of a visionary that I long to be able to enjoy this wonder without running the gauntlet of that preceding battle through ticket-counter queues, crowds, questioning, cross purposes, and the general mayhem common to all airports and here therefore reached the conclusion that the meanest sparrow is higher privileged than I and anyone?

The thought was crystallized in me in India when I joined the crowd collecting daily on a mountainous rock to wait for the two immense birds, at first mere specks on the far horizon, who every day at precisely the same hour, growing larger and ever more frighteningly beautiful, approached their midday meal, sailed downward with a controlled grace, pounced, speared the lump of meat with their beaks, wheeled round and were gone into the empyrean.

It was not their revolting menu I hankered after nor necessarily their disciplined punctuality insofar as mealtimes were concerned. I envied them their self-propelled power, their freedom, and their boundless world.

In short, I wish I were an eagle.

Tom Montague Meyer, C.B.E.

Industrialist, farmer, hospital chairman (Fleur Cowles's husband)

A bull: in the Sussex countryside, when I go round our herd of pure-bred Hereford cattle and look my new young bull, Tom, in the eye, there is a feeling of mutual respect.

He is docile, as all good Hereford bulls should be; he has been pampered since a calf, because even then he was obviously a future champion. Now in his prime, he has great strength, the best of care, the best of food—and forty beautiful Hereford wives! And he is the master of all he surveys!

James A. Michener

Author

I not only would like to, but I expect to return to earth shortly after my demise as an armadillo.

I have selected this delightful little creature for a wide variety of reasons. It is, to begin with, an adorable creature, the fancy of those who really love animals, the chosen creature of the cognoscenti, and a beast that has never done any human being or any other animal any harm.

It maintains a low profile, is not ostentatious, has a sense of humor, is kind to its children, is rowdy when having a good time, and is strictly nocturnal, so that when it does raise hell it is at a time when it disturbs no one.

One of its great attractions is that it is one of our oldest creatures, its ancestors dating far back toward the time of the dinosaurs. It is thus an emblem of survival on this earth, a problem that will begin to concern mankind as the destruction of human society looms.

It is an engineering marvel, its nine bands serving as a kind of natural accordion, its forefeet providing one of the best excavating tools in the world. Three armadillos can dig up your rose garden totally, in one night. But after some weeks, it can also become a responsive pet.

It is edible, serving during the Great Depression as Hoover Pig or Roosevelt Chicken, but my major interest in nominating it is a venal one that I must in all decency reveal. It is going to be one of the heroes of my next book so I want him to receive maximum attention now.

Sir John Mills

Actor

If I had to choose to come back in a new life as an animal I should plump, without any hesitation, to be a racehorse. I love to be pampered and patted and petted and beautifully looked after and so do they. I should make only one stipulation; and that is I would have to be the *best* horse. I have always been a great competitor and I should insist on winning all the classic races, particularly the Derby. I can think of nothing more exciting than being led into the winner's enclosure surrounded by an adoring audience. You can see by my choice that I am not the slightest bit conceited!

Vijaya Lakshmi Pandit

Indian high commissioner to the
U.K., 1955–61, also to Ireland and
Spain during the same period;
ambassador to the U.S.S.R., 1947–
49; president of the U.N., 1953–54

I was born a much-loved daughter of the Nehru. Health and happiness have been mine; opportunities and success that seemed impossible for a woman have opened out before me. All this is, no doubt, the result of merit acquired by me in a previous birth. But what will happen should I be born again? Another birth is inevitable because I am still far from Nirvana. Should it happen that my rebirth takes place in animal guise I would wish to be a part of the wildlife species, the jungle dwellers and, more important, that I be born an elephant—the most powerful of mammals today, descendants of earth's oldest inhabitants who roamed the land over fifty million years ago. Although extinct, man knew the mammoth, one of the forerunners of our elephant today.

In the wild state, the leader of the herd is a benevolent monarch, vegetarian but with a sweet tooth (wild elephants can create havoc if they get near a sugarcane field).

But Indian elephants are also hard workers. Our forest department uses them to work in jungles to shift heavy logs, clear impassable areas, and for transport in places where thick vegetation and "elephant grasses" make other transport difficult.

Elephants are also essential to prestige, pomp, and splendor. In the courts of princes they had a unique position, and even now India's many processions would be lifeless without the daily decorated and signified elephant who is often their main attraction. A richly caparisoned elephant is unrivaled in dramatic effect (once an essential of the panoply of royalty in India), taught how to walk in a royal procession and how to salute the maharaja.

The elephant also has a divine form in India—Ganesh or Ganpati, a human form and the head of an elephant. Known as the Lord of Obstacles, he protects and blesses the beginnings of ventures. He is a cheerful god, whose picture or statue is in every Hindu home—even tiny children know innumerable verses to Ganesh seeking his protection. His image is often worn around the neck for protection in the manner of the St. Christopher medallion worn by Christians. Elephants are loved and honored in India. They have been commemorated in art through the ages in magnificent stone temple carvings and in delicate miniatures. To Indians the elephant gives the feeling of being "man's best friend." If fate so wills, I think I might quite enjoy being an elephant!

Mollie Parnis

Fashion designer

The gazelle is my idea of a blissful incarnation. It is left alone in beautiful space and doesn't have to give parties.

A gazelle is so graceful, so divine. It stays thin and doesn't have to work for a living. A gazelle is one of nature's rare treasures, adorning the world yet seeing to it that people keep their distance.

Of course, a gazelle is not a political animal nor a media freak; I don't know how I'll manage without politics, TV, and the daily papers. Is there a species of gazelle called the gazette?

Sir Richard Parsons

U.K. ambassador to Sweden

I see myself as a greyhound, lithe and thin,
As I streak from the leash, the cheering will begin.
With frenetic speed, I shall hurtle round the course,
Even faster than a horse.

No ounce of surplus fat will mar my line,
My cholesterol level will be simply fine.
And my grateful backers will weekly render thanks
For the concentrated muscle power in my spindly shanks.

Julian Pettifer
TV journalist and presenter of natural-history films

To my mind, that vision of eternity that offers a paradise of harping angels seated on fleecy clouds appears infinitely more hellish than the fiery furnaces and the horned wildlife to be found in the other place. Hence, the only kind of immortality I care to contemplate is the possibility of reincarnation as another animal (even a human one); and if reincarnation it is to be, there is no question about the species. For a few moments I toyed with the idea of a future life as a flea, savoring the chance of inhabiting the fragrant and forbidden quarters of some delectable mortal. There was also the enticing possibility of being a real "fly on the wall" and satisfying a catalog of voyeuristic ambitions.

However, a few weeks ago, I was on a diving expedition in the Red Sea. Leaning over the bows of the good ship *Jenny III,* I saw that we had been joined by a school of dolphins—a dozen animals riding the bow wave of our vessel, diving, leaping, occasionally speeding off to circle around us, and only finally leaving us as we slowed to approach our anchorage. Certainly, the animals I watched did everything to suggest they were having a terrific time; racing the boat, racing each other, jostling and joking like boisterous schoolboys; it occurred to me that their opportunities for having fun are infinitely greater than ours. Their world is so much larger and so much more accessible.

Every dolphin on earth has an even greater freedom of movement than that tiny fragment of mankind we call astronauts has in ours. Compared with those of us who are *not* astronauts, the dolphin is as a gazelle exploring its territory in competition with a snail.

As I watched the dolphins on that Red Sea journey, I marveled at their speed and at the effortless way they kept pace with us; as if it suited them, they streaked ahead of us. I recalled reading an account by Jacques Yves Cousteau of a dolphin sighting that still strains one's credulity. Cousteau claims that as he stood on the deck of a new French battle cruiser doing speed trials and traveling over thirty-three knots, he noticed that the vessel had been *passed* by a school of dolphins that must have been swimming at a speed greater than fifty miles an hour. That is what I want to do. I am tired of tentative forays into the ocean encumbered by lead weights, rubber suits, and compressed-air cylinders; and I am equally tired of struggling against gravity with ageing limbs, shrinking muscles, and shortening breath. As a dolphin, I shall set out to explore the earth's largest living space and I shall do it under my own power. I shall travel freely over 71 percent of our planet's surface, that 139 million miles that is covered by the oceans. And like my dolphin friends in the Red Sea, I shall look up at those poor forked creatures floating in their tin cans, and I shall laugh.

Harold Prince

Broadway impresario

If I came back as an animal, it would be a dolphin. I like the sounds of their voices and smiles and invariable good nature and their shining intelligence, and, of course, they're graceful.

There's a hotel on Oahu called the Kahala Hilton and it's among our favorite places to vacation. There's a large pool for the dolphins and another for people—and the contrast is striking!

Mary Quant

Fashion and cosmetic designer

〜✕〜

I am not sure that I would like to come back in a new life at all. I am constantly surprised that I have survived this one quite happily; I seem to have had a lot of good luck, and another might be pushing it a bit. And from what I have seen of the lot of most animals, and particularly the way they are treated by humans, I don't think there is much to recommend being one of them. Except, perhaps, for my dog.

He is unusually fortunate, of course, in that he is loved to distraction by me and all of our household and very popular with everybody else—including people who do not usually care for dogs and by other dogs of both sexes as well.

He is an old English bobtail sheepdog of impeccable aristocracy, huge charm, and no brain; he would have made an excellent P. G. Wodehouse hero and, indeed, leads very much that sort of life even though our house is smaller than Blandings Castle.

Size is irrelevant to this enormous dog who is just as hungry after a big lunch as a small one and is convinced that our tiny shi-szu is his mother—or, at any rate, his Aunt Agatha. But because of his imposing dimensions no human or animal ever dares to speak crossly to him, and his abject cowardice goes unnoticed. A falling leaf will stimulate his baritone bark and a passing plane will unleash a contralto yodel capable of stopping wild horses in their tracks. But a confrontation with a small rabbit will send him bounding back to the safety of the house where he likes to watch the Dulux commercials on television. He is generous with his love and loyalty and no unkind thought has ever crossed his mind; nor, as a matter of fact, any thought at all. He likes going for walks, going to the hairdresser, and listening to Mozart. He doesn't notice the rain and sleeps through most of the winter. I think I would quite like to be him.

Cliff Richard

Singer

While I don't accept the reincarnation idea, I've always dreamed of being able to fly—to swoop off like a seagull from some lofty clifftop and hover effortlessly on warm air currents.

It's just a pity that I'm not too keen on fish or lice!

Duke of Richmond and Gordon

Pilot, painter, peer

A year before the Kaiser war, the small Eton-collared boys of Ludgrove prep school, then at Barnet, could often see strange sights—the pioneer airmen circling their pioneer airfield at Hendon about six miles away—frail-looking little craft, all canvas and wires accompanied by a modest buzz, more like the sound of a small motor mower than that breathless screech of the jets that so disturb us all today.

Very soon came World War II and zeppelins. With some rather frightened small boys from our attic dormitory window, I saw a great zeppelin alight, sinking aflame to its doom in a field at Potters Bar, two miles away. I went back to bed palpitating a little, but imagining, as only youth is able, that I was a pilot, and the thrill and glory of it all. I was air-crazy.

Not much later, I built from drawings in the *Boys' Own Paper* a "man-lifting" glider. After weeks of toil in my mail workshop, I hauled it up a precipitous side of one of the South Down valleys behind my home. I stood between the wings like Lilienthal, faced into the wind, ran—and jumped. My glider was a write-off, and what made it worse was that my parents thought it funny. I cried a little. But I was still air-crazy.

Now you ask me, when reincarnated, what do I want to be: fish, fowl, or four-footed?

A dog? What if its owner is one of these sporting types yelling and threatening it with a leash? Or an elephant, if you had a passion for tearing up trees, but life would be hard work, dangerous in the jungle and humiliating in a zoo. A pussycat? They say the night life is good, if noisy! Or a tiger? No thanks, too rough. Or a crocodile? Fancy swanning around all day in dirty water, trying to look like a log.

My answer is, "Please, God, make me a bird, and while at it I fancy being a gull if that is convenient. It's the air for me. I know of no joy more uplifting than to have flown a little open-cockpit plane all alone on a beautiful summer evening. Cruising around in no hurry, in and out a few lovely fleecy white clouds, the world below a neat mosaic of fields, forests, and follies of all sorts, people and cars like tiny toys.

As a gull, I'd be very much my own master (feeling sorry for birds like pheasants and partridges, poor chaps—regarded as "game," shot at by snobbish parties and ending up on a dish).

Seriously, to return from fantasy to human experience, it is a fact that for years I have enjoyed a lovely dream—that I am a human glider with arms outstretched as wings. I jump, rise, and soar, just like a gull, over a crowd of upturned faces. I sense that they are amazed at my flying ability, and not a little jealous. I never actually land, but the experience is so enchanting I wish I could dream it every night. Maybe my family motto should be, "Oh for the wings of a gull."

Joan Rivers

Comedian

If I were an animal, I'd like to be a tramp duck. Everyone could refer to me as a Quack on her back.

H.E. Selwa Roosevelt

Chief of protocol at the White House

and

Archibald Roosevelt

Former diplomat, banker

Nobleza is the quality in both humans and animals that I admire more than any other. I use the Spanish word because its English translation falls flat. "Nobility" is not quite the same. It implies titles and heredity; I am speaking of an intrinsic quality—a description of the heart and soul.

Thus, to answer Fleur's question—I start with that quality. In my new life as an animal I want to be a noble animal. The lion comes to mind, but it is too fierce. The tiger too, but it is too feline. The thoroughbred horse, but it is too nervous—a troubled spirit. The elephant, but it is sometimes awkward and ponderous.

No. Of all the animals I have known and admired, none have I loved more than a Siberian husky—shaggy, beautiful, a heart full of love, but strong and protective. These animals have elegant faces, full of class and breeding. They move gracefully, but not prissily. Their fur is luxurious and always clean; they have a lovely natural aroma. They are huggable and lovable; but not catlike. They have much pride; they do not kowtow; their love is deep and sincere and they never forget you. They are not fickle. They are tender and wise.

I would like to live in the country, but not in the cold

Siberia they originally came from. Let them be immigrants—
like my parents to America. Even a dog's life there is better
than almost any other place in the world!

> She chooses a Siberian husky
> Not something fierce, feline, or tusky
> Who's noble, furry, sweetly musky
> With belly white, top grayish dusky.
> She wants to keep her female gender,
> So may the Lord in me engender
> When I return again to earth
> Male husky genes before rebirth,
> And help me find her country home,
> Again together we can roam
> Somewhere, somehow, the paths of life
> As husky man and husky wife,
> I'll nuzzle her and nip her ear
> And love her as I love her here.

Kenneth Rose

Author, columnist, London
Sunday Telegraph

Eeyore, the "Old Gray Donkey" from *Winnie-the-Pooh*, would be my choice: a beast of noble though melancholy dignity, patient in adversity and an exponent of *laissez-faire* in a world of busybodies and scolds.

Eeyore also brought a sense of proportion to the art of letters: "This writing business. Pencils and whatnot. Overrated, if you ask me. Silly stuff. Nothing in it."

Mary, Viscountess Rothermere

Socialite

If I were to be born again as an animal, I should choose to be a cricket. It is said they are charming and carefree; such qualities wouldn't be amiss in a free spirit; which time, though, is difficult to choose. Perhaps in the ninth century in China, in Lin Yutang's translation of the ancient tale of the fierce fighting cricket. Perhaps less tiring would be Pinocchio's conscience, or the good-fairy cricket on Dickens's hearth who inspired forgiveness, or the one on Edward Lear's aged Uncle Algy's nose.

The cosy, comfortable house cricket stays near the fireplace waiting for cinnamon crumbs and singing at night. Milton called it "the resort of mirth." If one wants to discover the temperature Fahrenheit, the times a cricket chirps in fifteen seconds plus thirty-seven equals that.

When the time came for Mary Cricket to go to the land beyond the sun, my bone would be made into Queen Mab's whit and whenever *Romeo and Juliet* was shown, one would be remembered.

Baron Philippe de Rothschild

Grower of the world's finest wines

Metempsychosis

Second nature, innate,
When something inspires us
Fires us, no matter how briefly
To see what it is that intoxicates
Thrills us, however elusive

To be alive, to sympathize
In worshiping certain beasts
Tiger on track of antelope
The vulture gliding on high
That stops to dismember a fieldmouse
Elephant's cosy disdain
Smug in his elegant strength

Were it within my power
My thoughts would turn to
Those most discerning, the wisest
For whom three realms
Air, water, earth
Are familiar elements

Duck, gull, wild goose

Not easy to choose
Not on the whim of the moment
Spare me the pain of deciding

Were I to find myself

Duck, assuming its plumage
Sarcastic, ecstatic,
Delighting from pool to pool
To brood on quiet landscapes
Waggling beak nosing the ooze of the lakebed
Content with the pleasure I found there.

Gull on a wingspread of waves
From crest to crest
Weather eye open for fish
Guzzling the haul in the trough
Plowed by the wake of a steamer
Making precarious love
Tending the fledglings
Lulled by the surge
Wooed by the warmth of the sun

Wild goose
Reigning in infinite space
Able to seize from the seasons'
Change my changes of scenery
High on a bearing
Up in the unseen lattice of latitudes

Veering in to a shelter
Peace there, rest for the wings
Barely existing, surviving
Flying blind, Cupid,
Drawn by magnetic attraction
Golden dream of an egg

Still indecisive?
Surprise me! I'll draw the short straw.

H.R.H. Prince
Sadruddin Aga Khan

Special consultant to the Secretary
General of the U.N.,
and co-chairman
of the Independent Commission on
International Humanitarian Issues

Emperor penguins always struck me as a remarkable species; they are the custodians of the Antarctic, observing the
cupidity of men from different nations bent on the callous
plundering of an area that rightfully belongs to the animal
kingdom. Why should they and their fellow creatures pay
the price of a geopolitical game or become the first victims
of World War III?

Unlike man, that splendid bird has understood the bene-
fits of family planning. The emperor lays only one egg per
year which the males, unlike their chauvinistic human coun-
terparts, carefully nurse, balancing it on their webbed feet
for sixty-five days—and sometimes covering great distances
in the process.

They are impervious to the sub-zero blizzards and survive
the South Pole winters by consuming their protective fat layer
down to one third of their normal weight.

This, and regular exercise, keeps their waistline under
control. They will walk fifty miles with the greatest of ease,
chicks in tow, feeding their offspring for ten months, to fol-

low the receding ice cap in its seasonal flow. Adoptions are frequent and orphans always rejoin other families.

Last but not least, they are always impeccably dressed and never have to bother to pack a dinner jacket when they travel.

Lily Safra

Wife of international banker

If I might come back to this world, as an animal, I would like to be a dog—medium-sized—and also, if possible, with a sweet character. Why? Because, maybe, there will be a tiny chance that my grandchildren would adopt me for their children. Dear God, what a beautiful blessing it could be!

Moira Shearer

Former ballerina

Twice—in an unexpectedly personal way—animals have crossed my path. The first occasion was a dinner party in London. A few friends and the parents (Spanish father, French mother) of our hostess. Upstairs after dinner I became aware that the charming Frenchwoman was staring at me—for quite some time. Before this could be embarrassing she turned to her husband and said, "You know, if I was a lion *that* is how I would like a woman to look." I was tremendously flattered—what woman wouldn't be? And lionesses do look a shade boring with their fur-flat heads.

The second occasion was again a dinner party, this time in the Scottish borders. Great friends living in a beautiful Adam house helped to keep their central heating going through the winter by entertaining parties of grouse-shooting Americans. We were twenty round the dining table. The American on my left was giving me strong Hopalong, Republican stuff that always makes me noisily liberal. It was too much for him; he turned bright red, choked on his meat, and shouted, "You're like an ocelot—just like a little ocelot." Only of course he pronounced it "arse-a-lot."

It was cats again—why am I always seen as a cat? Even my husband calls me "Cat." I don't particularly like cats; I'm a dog person. Ideally I would like to be, and to be seen to be, a golden retriever. Waving, creamy coat; melting eyes; always smiling; noble, trusting, faithful. But my American friend was very definite and probably nearer the mark. So I accept it. I've since checked on ocelots and rather like them.

Many unpleasant catty ways, of course, but they are beautiful, graceful, and fast-moving and look amusing and wonderful, sprawling lazily, legs a-dangle, tail a-twitch, on the branches of trees. I can almost see myself like that.

David Shepherd

Wild-animal portraitist

I'd want to be an elephant so I could redress the harm humans do to them.

I have watched sixty jumbos cavorting in a river playing with their babies. We poison their waterholes with battery acid.

I have seen a mother elephant gently lifting her tiny calf out of a mud bath, using her tusks like a forklift truck. We mow them down with automatic weapons.

Jumbos are so gentle and wise. They don't drop bombs on each other. It's not the poor old elephant's fault that it carried a commodity that we will go to any lengths, however barbaric, to take from it to satisfy our insatiable greed. (In 1983, Japan alone imported the ivory equivalent of 8 percent of the world's remaining population of African elephants—no wonder they will soon be on the endangered list!)

Ivory really does look best on elephants. They are so much wiser and they are to be envied. They would so love to be left alone, to be allowed just to get on with the business of being elephants. Will we *ever* learn?

Ned Sherrin

BBC TV, theater star and producer

I would like to be a centipede. My legs are my only good feature, and if I come back I would love to have forty-nine more pairs.

Lord Sieff
of Brimpton

Merchant, philanthropist

If I came back in a new life as an animal I would like to be a horse.

The reason is simple; my daughter Daniela is a rather good rider. All I ask is that she should lavish on her mother and me, while we are alive as human beings, about a quarter of the care, attention, and affection that she lavishes on her horse.

Beverly Sills

General director,
New York City Opera

Oh, to be a giraffe who could sing!
Imagine the joy I could bring?
With my long neck and throat
I would hold a high note
And watch jealous birds take wing!

Wayne Sleep

Dancer, stage and TV performer

. . . the Loch Ness Monster, because without having to perform or even appear, he is always being filmed or televised.

Terence Stamp

Stage and screen actor

My God, Fleur, I don't want to come back, let alone as an animal. If I did get dragged on, with every phobia screaming resistance, it would only be with Silvana Magnano's looks, and a voice like Rosa Ponselle.

Ariana Stassinopoulos

Author

Next time, I want to come back as a butterfly. If I look back through my life, it's been a process of evolving from caterpillar to butterfly. And the process still goes on! Well, next time, I want to be *born* a butterfly—full-fledged and already flying. No hiding, no holding back in my cocoon, no feelings of contraction, restriction, limitation. No process. Just being. And flying. And freedom. Not life as a process of emerging from the cocoon, of getting free from images, beliefs, opinions, fears. But life as a state of being free, of being born already a butterfly. A purple-and-blue butterfly, forever soaring.

James Stewart

Actor

ꭟ

If I would come back in a new life as an animal, I'd want to be a dog . . . not a little dog and not a great big dog, but just sort of a middle-size dog like a setter or a golden retriever. I wouldn't want strict training when I was very young, and I wouldn't want to be taught to smell around and find bombs or criminals.

I wouldn't want to be lazy, but I would like to be with a family, and I would want them all to treat me as a part of the household. I wouldn't want them to spoil me, but then again I wouldn't want them to put me in a doghouse out in the backyard with a short chain. I would like to be able to come in the house, and I would like them to take me for a walk as often as they could.

I would like to be the kind of dog that knows when guests enter the house and be courteous to them, but I'd like to have a good solid bark so that a burglar would think twice about getting in.

I'd want my owners to be kind to me because, as I grow older, I'd learn how to be kind to them. I would like to grow old gracefully and, as the years went by, I'd learn what friendship means, and I'd like to become a good friend of the people I'm with.

Sting

Rock musician, actor

I'd choose to be a Yeti because at least then I would be able to prove to the world its existence . . . the Yeti really has fascinated me for years now and I'm hoping to organize a tracking expedition across the Himalayas sometime next year. Part of the trip will include a Yeti hunt.

Sir Roy Strong

Director, Victoria and Albert Museum, London

I do not know anything about the daily life of an ermine, but at least I would end up edging a ducal coronet or going to all the best places as part of a fur coat. Hermione Gingold once said that she had left her fur coat in her will to her sister and that she was worried about its future because it had always led such a glamorous life and was doomed in the future to a dull one. I fell in love with the ermine purely because one nestles on the sleeve of Queen Elizabeth I's dress in the famous Ermine Portrait at Hatfield House. It peers up, just as I would like to have done, at her face, and its tail is wrapped right round that sleeve, the darker tip emerging at the other side. It is a very superior ermine and has a beautiful golden collar around its neck set with diamonds and topazes—and all these things, animal included, symbolize her chastity. I am not sure that I would like to come back as an ermine, but I would certainly like to go backward as one. As a dazzling white-furred little beast, with or without my jeweled collar, I can be seen reclining on the arm of Leonardo da Vinci's portrait of a smiling lady and, in embroidered form on a banner, I appear in a hundred pictures of Petrarch's *Triumph of Chastity*. In the renaissance a king of Naples had as his device an ermine surrounded by a wall of mud—the animal preferring to perish rather than soil the purity of its coat. Yes, definitely, life as a bejeweled ermine, regal and snow-white, beautifully mannered, soft to the hand, a reminder to everyone in a tarnished world of a long-lost virtue. And the ermine bites too. . . .

Elizabeth Taylor

Actress

I think I would come back as a "jungle cat." I admire their beauty, their independence of character, but yet their dependence on each other as a group makes them very attractive to me. I also adore their freedom of spirit and their quickness of mind and body.

David and Martha Tiller
Flower designs, publicist

Cygnets—we should return as mute swans—beautiful, decorative, and graceful to swim forever on the quiet, still waters of your lake at Sussex—a "cob" and a "pen" to glide hopefully by royal decree for at least a century and then, as noted by the likes of Plato, Chaucer, and Shakespeare, to sing the loudest song before peace in death.

The Hon. Russell E. Train
CEO, World Wildlife Fund
Oh, to be an Elephant!

Of all the animals, great and small, terrestial or marine, that I have been privileged to observe in the wild, it is the elephant that I would most rather be!

A creature of great dignity and courage, the elephant is usually gentle although it can be terrible in its wrath when angered. It is surely the strongest beast that walks the earth. Elephants are affectionate and caring with one another, particularly when one is sick or wounded. Strong family ties exist between cow elephants and their offspring. Elephants are wise, and recent investigations by World Wildlife Fund researcher Katy Payne indicate that a complex and highly developed system of sound communication (inaudible to humans) exists among them. Dieting would not be a problem as I imagine an elephant can eat as much as it wishes. What joy!

Elephants have no serious predators, except man, to worry about, and if I were to get my wish to be an elephant, I would want a second wish: that my tusks be very small.

Twiggy

Actress

Most entertainers, from time to time, suffer from being misquoted and misused by the all-powerful and inventive press. The animal I would most like to re-enter the world as similarly has suffered from being misunderstood, with a fearsome image far removed from the reality of its gentle, unassuming life pattern.

My choice is the gorilla.

Not the macho, cigar-chewing, tight-faced, bereted, gunslinger kind that seems to delight in wars and disasters, but the non-U, massive hairy primate with the saddened eyes that have seen it all before, which knows the futility of aggression.

Gorillas are vegetarian (I am trying to be one), enjoy frolicking (me too, baby), and are only roused to fierceness when threatened or provoked (perhaps by the same reporter who always turns up at airports to interview me after a twenty-hour flight when I would rather have a hot bath than a warm photograph).

Gorillas come in three sizes, large, very large, and excuse me you're blocking my view of Mount Kilimanjaro.

The gorilla is not an elegant clotheshorse type of creature, but, with its own Bowery overcoat, there is no need for anything else, and anyhow I have seen and worn enough silks and raiments to last a lifetime, and certainly would not want to experience a new one wearing the same adornments. As a gorilla I might decide to curl my hair a little, although not to enter into competition with the lion, with whom I would expect to live in harmony, or in Timbuktu, or wherever, very peacefully.

Gorillas live in groups, usually one male with several females, and although not a great female libber, I would want to make the relationship more equal as I am not keen on sharing; of course I don't have a bra to burn.

Peter Ustinov

Actor, author, director, playwright

I wouldn't care much to be readily edible, even by gourmets. I went to a drama school where we had to be animals for one whole term. Most of the ambitious girls became gazelles and swallows, exhausting themselves for little purpose. The boys preferred macho creatures like tigers. Being lazy by conviction as well as by nature, I became a salamander, and lay perfectly still for four months, an expression of permanent glazed surprise on my face, occasionally flicking my tongue to show I was alive. I have not changed my opinion, even if I risk being found beneath a stone. I realize there are inconveniences, but they are distributed among the whole spectrum of choice. I may not make a good dish, but I might easily end my existence, to quote Lady Bracknell, as a handbag!

Robert Vavra

Photographer, author

To be born an animal
Makes me think at first of something small.
But a hummingbird though so ornate and fast
in this hostile world would hardly last.
Then what about something *big*,
say the size of a pig.
But who would want to awaken
and find one's self someone's bacon.
Then why not me?
The human animal.
In truth that's what I'd rather be.

Alexander Walker

Author, film critic

Given the choice, I'd like to come back as—a flea. There's safety in numbers, for the flea isn't a vanishing species. And there's safety in inconspicuousness, for fleas don't usually stand out in their habitats. Moreover, what a democratic little thing a flea is! It has no scruples on what (or whom) it makes its home. Yet it's not the sort of left-wing idealogue who feels at ease only in low company. Of all upwardly mobile creatures, the flea is the exemplar. Its prowess in this respect would also satisfy any ambition I cherish to be an Olympic champion: I suppose this is a hangover from those comics I read as a child which were always recording the "believe-it-or-not" exploits of man and mammal. Was it the height of the Empire State Building that a flea would jump in relation to its own size? I've forgotten, but I know it's high. Moreover, diminutiveness has its own attraction for me. To be small—to be very, very small—turns the familiar forms of the world into palpable wonderment. And to be able to *hop!* as one travels would be like finding those seven-league boots that were the boast of every good giant's closet in the fairy stories. As for food, well, that's a delicate matter; but I'm sure I wouldn't require very much—not like some creatures that have to eat twice their own weight every hour or expire from famine. Fleas must have very small appetites—there'll be enough to go round. I daresay for all their closeness to humanity, fleas have none of the traditional loyalty of dogs; for all their ability to move fast, they have none of the streamlined grace of cats. They are, though, performers that take to training more easily than cats and behave more impeccably than dogs; and take up a smaller space than either dogs or cats. I feel, as a flea, I'd be good at acrobatic tricks and wouldn't have any humane society getting exercised on my behalf. I'd have *fun.* Only one thing worries me—how would Fleur ever work me into a painting of hers? I don't suppose there'll be a place in that modern Noah's Ark she's pledged to fill with the "Top of the Animal Pops"; my only hope would be to sneak in, under cover, so to speak, on some friendly hide or fur. The artist's keen eye might spot me, but what could she do with a fellow my size? Only one thing, I fear . . . dear Fleur, how's your *pointilliste* technique?

Barbara Walters

Journalist,
ABC News, New York

My first reaction is that I would like to come back as a small dog, perhaps a little French poodle. It seems to me they have wonderful lives. They are petted and catered to, and usually very much loved. They are fed chopped sirloin, usually sleep on soft white pillows, and, in general, lead the kind of lives few people do. So that's it for me—I want to be a small French poodle named Fifi.

Robert White

Tenor

If I could choose to come back, the *first* thing that comes to mind (and it has *always* been on my mind) is to be a quail! I like the fact that, in a somewhat unassuming way, they can still attract so much attention, especially with the little crest on their head that says, "Hey! Look at me! Watch what I can do!"

As a quail, I would still be known for my song. In a few states, especially the southern ones, I would even be called by its song which is, in fact, my own name, "Bob White." I would be reminded of my own youth, and my own love of singing for and entertaining people—the other Bob White.

Often, on television, I have been summoned to sing. In the next life I wouldn't be called by name—rather, by the whistle of the distinctive "Bob White" call. Leonard Bernstein does all this.

Peregrine Worsthorne

Editor,
London *Sunday Telegraph*

My first choice would be an elephant, in the hope that reincarnation in that shape would at long last endow me with a good memory. A gadfly would be acceptable as a second choice, since this would mean my being able to continue to do what comes naturally to a journalist. (A sloth would also require, for me, little change of character.) Generally speaking, the most disagreeable aspect of being any kind of wild animal would be the need for remaining constantly on the alert against predators, even when asleep; never being able to relax or take a holiday away from all the worries involved in staying alive. So to avoid all that anxiety, I think I might choose to be a lady's lapdog on one condition: that I should have some say in the lady in question.

Michael York

Actor

ᗞᕮ

I would like to come back as a parrot—in particular as a domesticated one with bright plumage and a saucy eye perched in the warmth and comfort of some loving household, rather than as a sad lifer behind bars in some alien zoo. As a parrot one would be the instant center of attention and would never have to go far for food or conversation. All parrots are great dandies, but they also have some otherworldly quality, perhaps derived from their ability to "talk" to humans. I know that other birds can do this, but the mynah bird, for example, all squawk and squirt, lacks the parrot's essential dignified *gravitas.* Moreover, parrots are reputed to live to a great age—no fleeting mayfly existence for them—and it would be fun to witness at first hand the extraordinary developments that the twenty-first century will inevitably bring to the world. And in this graying world of shrinking jungles and increased pollution, a parrot would lend an essential color, charm, and humor, and maybe even a few words of wisdom!

P.S. I have to confess that perhaps my choice of afterlife animal is inspired by a letter from a fan. She claimed that her parrot has become so fond of the signed photograph that I had sent her—which, for some unaccountable reason, she had put in its cage—that it would shriek with rage at any attempt to remove it. It would apparently become even more moved if I appeared on the television and would swoop round the room in high-pitched ecstasy. In any incarnation, one couldn't hope for greater devotion . . . !